The Forgotten
CONTRACT

The Forgotten CONTRACT

Eugene Papp

WestBow
PRESS
A DIVISION OF THOMAS NELSON

WestBow Press books may be ordered through booksellers or by contacting:

WestBow Press
A Division of Thomas Nelson
1663 Liberty Drive
Bloomington, IN 47403
www.westbowpress.com
1-(866) 928-1240

ISBN: 978-1-4497-8583-3 (sc)
ISBN: 978-1-4497-8582-6 (e)
ISBN: 978-1-4497-8584-0 (hc)

Library of Congress Control Number: 2013903099

Printed in the United States of America

WestBow Press rev. date: 3/29/2013

The danger of success is that it makes us forget the world's dreadful injustice.

—Jules Renard

The real test of a man is not how well he plays the role he has invented for himself, but how well he plays the role that destiny assigned to him.

—Jan Patocka

Man in the Arena

It is not the critic who counts: not the man who points out how the strong man stumbles or where the doer of deeds could have done better. The credit belongs to the man who is actually in the arena, whose face is marred by dust and sweat and blood, who strives valiantly, who errs and comes up short again and again, because there is no effort without error or shortcoming, but who knows the great enthusiasms, the great devotions, who spends himself for a worthy cause; who, at the best, knows, in the end, the triumph of high achievement, and who, at the worst, if he fails, at least he fails while daring greatly, so that his place shall never be with those cold and timid souls who knew neither victory nor defeat.

—Theodore Roosevelt

Nobody's Friend

My name is Gossip. I have no respect for justice. I maim without killing. I break heart and ruin lives. I am cunning and malicious and gather strength with age. The more I am quoted, the more I am believed. My victims are helpless. They cannot protect themselves against me because I have no name and no face. To track me down is impossible. The harder you try, the more elusive I become. I am nobody's friend. Once I tarnish a reputation, it is never the same. I topple governments and wreck marriages. I ruin careers and cause sleepless nights, heartaches and indigestion. I make innocent people cry in their pillows. Even my name hisses. I am called Gossip. I make headlines and headaches.

Before you repeat a story, ask yourself: Is it true? Is it harmless? Is it necessary?
If it isn't, don't repeat it.

—author unknown

Introduction

This story is about a long forgotten request that I'd asked of the spirit world in the fall of 1952. It turned out to be a contract for all practical purposes; I just didn't realize it then, and I forgot about it as soon as I made it. I did not realize that it would be fulfilled. In hindsight, it was for the best that I'd forgotten about it.

I was an ignorant, undereducated young man of nineteen years living on a farm and totally unfamiliar with the relationship between the human race and the spirit world—and about life in general. I did not realize the power of the spirit world and the seriousness of the forces that I set into motion at that time. This required correction at any cost and under any circumstances. The forces beyond the seeable world—the spirit world—were requesting it. It was depending on me, and I did not realize that until it ran its course.

There is a saying: "Be careful what you ask for; you might get it." I have experienced this. We wish for or ask for something and then forgot about it as time goes on. We may wonder, many years later, why certain things happened to us and who or what had caused these things. This story is about the search for correction in my memory.

I've wanted to write about it several times, in spite of the fact that the spirits told me not to write about it until I am an old man. Every time I've tried, a fear has gripped my mind and I've had to abandon my efforts.

My father from the spirit world got in touch with me in the fall of 2009 and explained to me that I'd made my request the wrong way. I shouldn't have done it the way I did. What would

I have done if I'd become asthmatic, like he was? I would have had a very difficult time in school. The risks never really entered my mind. How differently should I have done it? I really do not know.

The spirit world got in touch with me again in January 2010 and informed me that I did not thank them for their help. The fear that I'd previously experience when I'd attempted to write about my experience was removed at this time.

Therefore, I am expressing my thanks from my heart and from my mind to the spirit world of István Kaszap and his associates for their help. I am extremely grateful to the spirit world for the way they've treated me and my request. It was all up to them, and I do not know if it could have been done any better.

Chapter 1

Unforeseen Events

When an incident like a birth of a child or an animal takes place, the entire body of the mother prepares to handle the event. Long before any other incident occurs in nature, all the supporting events are ready to go into action.

In hindsight, this process of preparing for the future is why I had to fail a test to make my departure from Hungary easier. It was a laboratory exam given at the end of my spring semester in 1956. What I had to do could not be done in Hungary. I am sure there are people who will disagree with me. But then again, they don't have my life experience. They do not have the same needs as I do. They travel on a different personal journey.

The instructor was from my area of the country. He told me he could give me a passing grade but wouldn't do it because I was smarter than that. I did not reply, because I knew the problem: I misunderstood the main question on the test. Unfortunately, I could not take a second test because I had to go to military service during the summer. Therefore, I would have to repeat quantitative analytical chemistry.

I spent part of the summer, July of 1956, in the military service and August in my hometown. I returned to my dormitory in September. At the time I had two girlfriends living together in an apartment in the city. One of them worked in a lock factory.

She asked me to come to her company's employment office and apply for a job. They were hiring two people in the heat and steam generating area. So, I applied and got a part-time job, since I was going back to school in the spring. I was assigned to report to an older employee who was going to teach me all the ins and outs of the system. My first day was to be November 1, 1956. Yet, it was never meant to take place.

That summer I heard rumors about some changes some people wanted to see from the government, but nothing concrete. I was not informed or involved in any of the planning. However, what would happen because of this affected me in a very real way.

I had been visiting my lady friends on the evening of October 23, 1956. I was coming back to the dormitory at about eleven o'clock in the evening and got off the streetcar near the radio station. I was surprised to see a crowd and tanks around the radio station. Only then did I hear about what had taken place earlier in the evening.

I was told that the state police fired into the demonstrators who'd wanted to go into the radio station and broadcast something. I spent a few hours amid the crowd, and at around two in the morning I headed back to the dormitory. A few days later I was asked by some students to join them in becoming part of a supporting police force of Imre Nagy. Armed with submachine guns, two other students and I walked around the city of Budapest.

One of my classmates was a member of the Communist Party and heard about the uprising. As he absorbed the news, he passed out and slid off his chair under the table. Some of the other students took him to the hospital a couple of blocks away, where he was given a tranquilizer injection to sedate him. Sadly, he still had not recovered a month later. I do not know whether he ever recovered.

One day we were called to one of the railroad stations. There were several restricted rooms where the state police kept records of all the people who illegally left Hungary. There was an invading force of the Soviet army sent in to suppress the uprising. A battle ensued between the Soviet army and the Hungarian military forces on Jozsef Circle Road. The Hungarian artillery forces destroyed many Soviet military vehicles. I saw body parts hanging from tree branches and unexploded mortar shells sticking out of the middle of the road where our dormitory was located. They were halfway embedded in the road. But soon the Hungarian military forces appeared to repel the Soviet forces, at least temporarily.

A few days later, the invasion of the Soviet army came. A group of T-34 tanks were moving in. Machine guns were mounted on the backs of trucks, and soldiers were shooting at buildings and people. One lady got shot in the buttocks, and one young boy was bleeding from his mouth. I picked him up and noticed that he had a bullet wound in his chest. We put him on a motorcycle behind the driver and wrapped a rope around him and the driver; he was whisked away to the hospital. We went back to the dormitory after that, because the Soviet army was moving in with a large force.

The dormitory I lived in was a large U-shaped building. The basement of this building also served as the dining facility for the medical school. There was an open area before the entrance of the dormitory where five steps led up to the entrance. A receptionist cubicle stood on the left side as one entered the building.

As we entered our dorm, one of the Soviet T-34 tanks came up into that open area. About ten of us students were inside the door and could see that the tank was raising its cannon. We thought that it was going to shoot at us, therefore we ran to the end of the hallway on one side and hid behind a corner. Then we heard a shot. The shells exploded, destroying the receptionist cubicle and the wall separating it from the hallway. We all would have been killed had we not ran to the end of the hallway.

Once quiet settled on the area, we looked out the window of

a room and saw the tank pulling away. The soldiers in the tank probably thought we were all dead. We did not come out while the tank was in sight. A short time later, the members of the state police were running around looking for people with guns. The guns we had were put away by a superintendent in a pile of coal in the basement of an apartment. I have no idea what he did with them after that.

A day or two later, I was going to visit a relative when I heard a lot of commotion coming from a side street. There were about ten people, mostly women, stomping on something. I went closer and saw two or three Soviet soldiers on the ground dead. I have no idea how they died, but the women wore high heels and their legs were bloody. It was a gruesome sight. The soldiers were from an armored car that was standing nearby. The hatred toward the Soviet army was shown with those women's actions.

Eventually the Soviet army moved in with force and shot at buildings and people and took over the city. Two of my friends and I saw some Soviet soldiers standing near the Danube River, and they thought it was the Suez Canal. One of them was pointing to the river saying, "Suez, Suez." Apparently, they did not know where they were. They may have been scheduled to go to Egypt because of the British and French attack on the Suez Canal.

Most of the students went home after the uprising was suppressed. But others were stuck at the school. There were about two hundred pounds of lard and ten thousand pounds of potatoes stored in the basement. So for many of us, our diet consisted of fried potatoes in lard and water for a few weeks. I distributed some of the lard and potatoes to people I knew who had no food. Ten children who ran away from an orphanage also showed up at the dormitory. We fed them and let them sleep in the dining room on the floor. The people we fed were happy to get food and some even gave me money for helping them. I spent some of the money on two suits.

I made a decision around the middle of November to go home

and get out of the country. I left all my belongings in my room in the dormitory and took only the suit I had on and my raincoat and identification documents. A friend and I wanted to go to Austria, so we took the train one evening to Körmend and left Budapest permanently behind. The final destination of the train was a city at the corner of Austria, Hungary, and Yugoslavia. We met a ticket checker on the train, and she just happened to be from my village. I asked her to show my friend where he could get off and easily cross the border to Austria. I did not want him to come with me, because I did not know what I was going to do.

The train arrived at Körmend about nine the next morning, and I proceeded to walk to my village. There were many Soviet soldiers in Körmend. While I was passing through the bridge of the Rába River, a truck came and stopped next to me. There were three people in the cab. They asked me where I was going, and I told them my destination. The driver said, "Hop in the back. We are going to the village next to yours."

We got to about five hundred meters before my house, and the truck could not go up the hill. The back of the truck was too light and the wheels were spinning. The driver of the truck told me they were unable to get up the hill and they were going to turn back. I got off and walked the rest of the way home.

My parents and my brothers were surprised to see me coming home. A young boy, who'd been in the custody of the state, used to live with my grandparents in the village. The state had moved him to a school in Budapest at the age of sixteen. He'd seen me in the city during the uprising. He went back to the village and told everybody that I was carrying a gun when he saw me. My family was urging me to get out of the country. I got drunk a couple of times over the next few days and played cards with friends. I was home for about ten days.

Chapter 2

Leaving Hungary for the United States

One of my friends in the village was in the army but was home because of the revolt. He did not want to go back to the army and was asking me to get out of Hungary with him. He had relatives in the village of Ivánc, near the border. Around twenty people from Ivánc were planning to get out of Hungary during the first week of December.

My friend and I rode our bicycles to Ivánc on the designated day. At around eleven o'clock that night, as a group we walked across the Rába River barefooted and carrying our shoes about our neck. The water where we crossed was slightly above the knee and fast moving. The river was deeper in other parts. We were holding hands and had to move fast, because when we took a step the water would wash the gravel away from under our feet. We all made it across and put our shoes back on. There was about five hundred yards of farmland between the river and a highway. We would just have to cross the highway and a set of railroad tracks, and after a few hundred yards we could cross the Austrian border.

We were getting close to the highway when suddenly gunfire erupted and flares went up in the air, illuminating the land. There were many Soviet trucks and some tanks on the road. The soldiers were yelling to the people to come to the road, and they were shooting up more flares. Two men from Ivánc and I started running away. I said to myself, *You will have to shoot me to stop me.* We met up at the bank of the river. One of the men said that he knew of a small wooden boat that was tied out on our side of the river; we decided to take it back across the river, and he would return it the next day. That is what we did.

I slept at one of the men's houses and rode my bicycle back home the next day. The Soviet army took all the people they captured to the police station in Körmend. My friend was taken back to military service. My father asked my friend if he knew where I was. He told my father that I had not been caught by the Soviet army but he did not know where I was. It was late in the afternoon when I got home; my family was happy to see me.

I had another friend whose sister's in-laws lived right on the Austrian border. Two of us rode our bicycles to this town three days after the Ivánc border crossing failed. We were stopped by the Soviet army three times to check our identification, which was required for people who lived in the area to go within fifty kilometers of the Austrian border. We both had our permits since we hadn't given up our permanent residency when we'd moved to Budapest. It looked to us as if the Soviet army was expecting an invasion from the west, because they had cannons pointing toward the Austrian border.

My friend Steven and I walked across the border to Austria late that evening, December 12, 1956. We were picked up by members of the village police department as soon as we entered Austria. They took us to the village fire station, where they had temporary accommodation for all the refuges coming from Hungary across the border. There were about six other Hungarian people there who had crossed the border a few days before.

A man from the village came to the firehouse and asked us if we wanted to help him split firewood. He lived with his mother, and they had been Hungarians before the First World War. We split wood for them for four days. She gave each of us a dollar, since we were planning to go to the United States. He took us to his wine cellar on two evenings, and we evaluated his different wines. We had a great time. He told us a story about a young female high school teacher. She'd had sex with all twenty of her students, and she got pregnant. All the students had to pay child support to her after the baby was born. We spent about seven days in the village.

We were picked up by a bus and transferred to Graz. My friend and I separated there. He went with the regular crowd looking for work, and I went with the students looking for chances to finish our studies. All the students were transferred to Gröbming, up in the mountains, two days later. Gröbming is located at the base of a scenic mountain by a brook. We were placed in a vacation hotel. Three of us adventurous students were going up the side of the mountain one day. We were about two hundred yards from the edge of the forest when suddenly we hear the sound of whistles and three people calling us back. The mountain did not look steep going up, but when we turned back it looked quite steep. The three people explained to us that winter storms developed very suddenly on the mountain and we could easily get lost in the forest and not find our way back. So we abandoned the mountain climbing project. We spent the Christmas holiday and about two additional weeks there.

We were transferred to Salzburg around the beginning of 1957. There we had to fill out several different types of documentation. We had to select the top three countries we would like to go to. I chose the United States first, Australia second, and Canada third. We had to have a sponsoring agency before we'd be able to go to any country. These agencies were responsible for helping people assimilate into the culture of the country. I was sponsored by the World Wide Catholic Charity organization. I had a cousin named William Papp who was living in Fairfield, and his mother was living in Bridgeport, Connecticut. I am not sure if that had anything to do with me being accepted into the United States; I think it must have, though, because my friend went to Canada. My relatives did not know that I was coming, and I really didn't want to be a burden.

All the refugees who were going to the United States were taken by train to Bremerhaven, where we boarded a US Navy transport ship—a troop carrier named *General Eltinge*—and headed toward the States. I got seasick two days later, when the boat hit the open sea, and was sick for about five days. I don't think I would have made a good sailor. It took about ten days to travel to New York City, where we arrived on January 31, 1957. We spent a night in a hotel in the city, and a day later we were taken by bus to Kemp Kilmer New Jersey.

All the students had to fill out applications for scholarships. These applications were handled by the World University Service. Copies of our applications were sent to different universities for evaluation. I was accepted to Columbia University in New York City. They gave me a date in September 1957 when I had to report to the university.

In the late February, we were transferred to Georgetown University in Washington, DC, to study English for three months. We lived in the university dormitory. We took canoe rides on the Potomac River, visited Mount Vernon (where George Washington had lived), and we went to the Arlington National Cemetery. I met several Hungarians families who lived in the area. After school was over, I lived with one Hungarian family for two weeks and then another family for two weeks while I was job hunting. Finally, I got a job working for the General Outdoor Advertising Company, and I was able to rent a room for myself. My job was to help them clear the land where they were putting up advertising boards or clear overgrown weeds around previously placed boards. This was the job where I got familiarized with poison ivy. It was a great experience. The people whom I worked with were trying to tell me not to go into the poison ivy–covered bushes. But I could not comprehend what they were talking about. I came down with the effects of poison ivy all over my body. I had the greatest itch of my life, but I was told not to scratch. I took hot showers when I should have put ice and cold water on the irritated area. The company sent me to a doctor, who gave me some pink solution that I had to rub on the affected area. It took about fourteen days to recover from it. There was an uncomfortable itch remaining on my rump after the poison ivy rash resolved. I suffered with it for more than a year before seeking further treatment. Several doctors prescribed more pinkish solutions, but it never got better.

The date to report to Columbia University was approaching, so I quit my job at the advertising company, gave up my room, and went to New York during the first week of September.

Chapter 3

Columbia University

I had a one-year scholarship for free tuition with room and board to Columbia University in New York City. I was also receiving one hundred dollars a month from the World University Service for living expenses. I got a part-time job at the university with the art and architecture department in October. The students were putting their designs and paintings on display for evaluation by the faculty. My job was to put the students' paintings and drawings into storage after their evaluations and make them available if needed for a second evaluation.

I lived in a double occupancy room on the first floor of one of the dormitories at the university. I had a roommate who was from Ansonia, Connecticut. As far as I can remember, this was his second year studying psychology at the university. All of his educational expenses were paid by the United State government because of his military service. He'd spent four years in the air force, most of it in Japan. I learned a lot from him about the culture in the United States and some about the Japanese culture he was familiar with. He liked to eat Japanese food, and we had a few dinners together at the nearby Japanese restaurant on Broadway.

He invited me to his parent's house for Thanksgiving day and also for Christmas day. They had a wonderful spread of food on both occasions, and I slightly overate. I had a great time at their house. His father was a salesman, and his mother was a stay-at-home mom. He had two brothers and a sister. One of his brothers was a pilot in the air force. He and his family were nice people. He made friends easily and had many friends at the university. It probably had something to do with his military service, or maybe it was just a talent he had. One of his friends got me hooked on eating chocolate-covered doughnuts and drinking beer. He and his friends played poker in the dormitory several times. I did not know anything about the game, so I only watched them.

There were many girls with average, good, and very good looks around the university. I remember one very good-looking girl from Texas. She was a nice person—probably the yellow rose of Texas. I liked her very much. My roommate and I talked a lot about the opposite sex, because he liked them and I liked them too. My roommate liked girls with big busts. There was a girl from Cuba in one of my English fall semester classes. She had about a forty-four-inch bust. He kept asking me to introduce him to her somehow. One day we arranged for him to accidentally meet us so I could introduced him to her. I do not remember how it turned out afterward.

A young Japanese man and two very good-looking Japanese girls were in one of my classes. They were all from the same city in Japan and from wealthy families. The father of the young man and one of the girls owned manufacturing companies; the other girl's father was a banker. They did not live on the campus. The girl with the banker father liked me a lot, and I really liked her too. We used to walk around campus together, and she would have me put my hand into her coat pocket so we could hold hands.

There was a big difference between us in regard to our financial situations. She could buy anything she wanted, and I could hardly keep up with my everyday needs. The three of them used to come over to my dormitory, and we would talk in the lobby about Japan and Hungary and our different cultures. The differences in our cultures and our finances were my biggest relationship concerns—mostly about her having money and me lacking money. I realized that under no circumstances could this romantic relationship go anywhere. We just had some fun. I still wonder whatever happened to her. Maybe I was sensing the difficult road that was about to unfold for me.

I was studying only English during the fall semester of 1957. I had to learn enough English to be able to understand scientific lectures in order to continue my education. The first semester went without any problems or any major events. I registered for about thirty credit hours in chemistry, physics, mathematics, and English for the second semester.

I had a class called Everyday English Communication on Tuesday evenings from 6:00 to 9:00 p.m. We had to bring that day's copy of the *New York Times* to each class. We studied how the newspaper reporters wrote the articles and how to understand them correctly. The reporters always wrote in a concise form so everybody could understand them and they could sell more papers. We learned about the usage of different idioms, the usage of words, and the everyday usage of written American English. All the students in this class were foreigners. About half of them were immigrants who needed to learn the Yankee language, as the teacher used to call it. The other half were just studying in the United States and were planning to go back to their homelands.

The second time the class met was in late January 1958. The weather was cold and snow covered the ground. There were about twenty people in the class. We had a half-hour break, and two people went out for coffee. I liked to drink coffee, so I ordered a large cup of black coffee with sugar. After the break, we started on the second half of the three-hour class. We were about halfway through the second half when some strange things begin to happen to me.

I became extremely nervous and fearful. My hand and my body started to shake. An enormously terrifying feeling came over me. I had to hold my right hand down with my left hand to be able to scribble, since the writing was almost impossible for me due to the shaking of my hand. A lady sitting next to me wanted to ask me something, but I had to brush off her question. I could not possibly talk to anyone. I had to concentrate on my work to avoid panicking. There was no evident reason why this was happening. I did nothing to cause it. I had no thought in my head that would have caused the fear. This lasted for about fifteen to twenty minutes and then was gone as suddenly as it came. I felt fine afterward.

The class ended, and we all went our separate ways. I went back to my room in the dormitory. My roommate called me shortly after I got in my room and asked me to bring him and another friend of ours some coffee. He was working part-time for the university a few nights during the week, liquefying helium in the physics building.

I went over to a nearby restaurant on Broadway, picked up coffee for the three of us, and went over to see them at about nine thirty. They asked me about the class I'd just had and if there was anything new otherwise.

"Well, there is really nothing I could tell you about," I said. I gave them their coffee, and we all started to drink. I'd only had a few sips of my coffee when the warm sensation started coming over me again. I went to the men's room, as if something was directing me to go there. I do not know why. The warm sensation was getting stronger. I took off my coat and started to wash my face and head with cold water. I felt I needed to do this to cool my body. After a few minutes, the warming sensation got much more intense. I took my shirt off and started to wash my upper body with cold water. I needed to cool my body to stop the sensation that I was experiencing. As I was throwing water over my neck and chest, the door opened quietly. A gentle-looking, light-complexioned black man who was about five and half feet tall came in and said to me, "Come. I will take you to where you can take a shower."

I grabbed my coat and picked up my shirt and followed him. He took me to an upper floor to a men's locker room. I assumed he was an employee of the university because he was familiar with the building. There were three parts to the locker room: the locker area, the sinks and toilet section, and about ten shower units in another area. I quickly undressed and started to shower. Being January, the water was very cold and it felt good. Just about then, all problems broke loose in my mind. A fear of unbelievable magnitude came over me. I had to turn the shower to full blast to cool my body. In fact, I had to turn on four of them and point the showerheads toward my body, because I felt like I was going to pass out. It felt that my brain was shutting down and I was going to collapse. My legs did not want to move. I was slapping them hard and kept yelling to my legs, "Move, legs, move!" They were getting numb from the cold water. I was doing push-ups, jumping up and down, and doing all kinds of exercises under the shower to try to avoid passing out. I could no longer see myself in the mirror that was hanging on the wall. The wall started fading away. The thought that I was losing my eyesight was terrifying me. "I am not going, I am not going," I said a few times. I do not know why I said it.

I do not remember if I ever lost consciousness or spent some time unconscious on the floor. I do not remember falling down or getting up. One probably doesn't remember that sort of thing, anyway. Sometime later, the man who took me up to the locker room came back. He glanced at me and said with surprise in his voice, "Are you still here?"

"Yes," I said. He asked me no more questions, which I was grateful for. He quickly left and did not come back again, at least not while I was there. I do not remember seeing him again. I must have had a terribly frightened look on my face, because he did not seem to want to look at me. I do not know what he thought of the situation. I do not know who he was, where he came from, or where he went. I do believe now that he was sent by some greater forces to assist me.

I tried several times to stop showering and go into the other part of the locker room, but within seconds the fearful panicky feeling would return. I was out of energy and cold when the feelings finally stopped. The clock in the locker room showed 2:00 a.m. I'd spent about four long hours taking a cold shower, trying to stay alive. Surprisingly I did not come down with a cold. It did not leave any ill effect in me with the exception of being very tired. I did not know why it happened or what was to come.

I got dressed and went back to my friends. They asked me, "Where the heck were you? Do you know what time it is?"

"Yes, I know what time it is! I was around the building," I told them. I did not tell them where I had been. I did not want them to know what had happened to me earlier in the evening. I'd heard of people putting LSD or other drugs into unsuspecting peoples' coffee. The thought occurred to me that someone put something in my coffee, but it was not possible since all three cups of coffee were poured from the same container in the restaurant and my two friends did not have any ill effects. After my roommate finished his work, we went back to our rooms and went to sleep.

I have learned over the years what this incident probably was. The spirits were triggering the kundalini force in my body. I had to be in the cold shower to prevent my body from catching on fire and suffering spontaneous combustion. Personally, I think the spirits came to remind me that the contract had to be canceled.

Chapter 4

Communication

I was exhausted, so I slept well that night. I did not come down with a cold or a fever. The only effect this left in me was that, for many years to come, I always wanted to be near where I could take a shower in case the fear came back. It never came back.

The next morning, a few hours after I'd woken up, I received the surprise of my life. I had company; some unseeable beings were talking to me. I'd never experienced anything like this before. I did not know where they had come from or why they'd come. At the time, I didn't think about whether this experience had anything to do with what had happened the night before.

I no longer remember exactly how it started out or how I realized that someone or some spirits were communicating with me; after all, this happened around fifty-three years ago. The voices were not really sounds. They did not seem to vibrate the eardrums. I did not have to turn or look around to see if anybody was there talking to me. The voices came through the audio nerve system. I was able to differentiate between actual sounds and the sounds that appeared to be forming in the nerves of my ear. There was a distinct difference in perception between the two forms of hearing. These sounds did not interfere with my hearing when someone was talking to me. If I was talking to someone or someone was talking to me, the spirits were silent. It was also not as if I was mentally talking to myself about something. Many people classify this as "hearing voices." I classify it as a mental communication rather than hearing voices. It also was not telepathic communication from another human being; I was somewhat familiar with that and could tell that this was different.

I may not have all the events in exact chronological order concerning how the communication events were taking place since so much time has passed. As far as I remember, they told me the first day that they were from the spirit world. What they did not tell me was the reason for the communication. They did not say and I did not ask how many of them there were, but they were communicating with me one at a time. They spoke mostly English and sometimes Hungarian.

Once the voice asked me to go to the store and buy cigarettes. *Why should I go and buy more, when I already have cigarettes?* I thought to myself. I usually had two packs in my pocket. But the voice insisted that I had to go and buy cigarettes and actually ordered me to do it. I went and bought cigarettes. The next time they told me to go buy coffee. Another time they told me to go to watch television in the dormitory and a few other things, such as go outside and take a breath of fresh air—nothing detrimental, nothing dangerous. Sometimes they made fun of me in a good-natured way. Sometimes they talked about old Hungarian jokes that I knew. They were trying to make my life more humorous at times. There were other small talks between the spirits and me early on, but I do not remember all the details. Some of these communications did not make much sense to me, but I went along with them. I had to go along; I had no other choice.

The communication from me to them was in thought form. They were reading my mind. When I made a decision about something, they seemed to know it. I could ask questions in thought form and get answers to some of my questions, but not to all. I never felt the need to use verbal communication with them.

I was curious and asked them, "How can you project thoughts into my brain?"

"Easily!" the spirits said. "It is done with something like radar waves, electromagnetic waves. You are not yet able to understand it. There is space, and the space is filled with different sizes of particles of matter. This particle system is where the electromagnetic waves travel. We can project the electromagnetic vibration carrying information into an individual person's brain.

The life in that particle system, the spirit world, is the real life as opposed to life on planet earth.

This particle system is outside the rules of physics as we know it. Teleportation of objects are taking place with the rules or laws of the particle system. These particles are the prime matter that the world around us is made out of, but how it is made I have no idea."

They were right; I really did not understand it. I had no workable concept of how all these thing were made up. What were the relationships of these spirits to the materialistic world we lived in? Human bodies have restricted degrees of freedom. The spirit beings have many more degrees of freedom. I really could not imagine the structural existence of the spirits and their world at that time.

We didn't discuss the distance between them and the human being when communication takes place. We also didn't talk about their life span in that particle system. I assumed that they were all around us and had very, very long life spans, because it is not a rapidly decaying particle system. Why did I assume that? I do not know.

They stated, "We know everything that you've done and what is recorded in your brain."

Great, I thought. *Just what I never wanted.* The things I wanted to keep secret from everyone in the world weren't secrets to them at all.

The spirits said, "We are here to stay." But they did not say why.

Welcome to my world. Make yourself at home, I thought to myself.

They never claimed to be Gods or God related. They never gave any names or affiliation with any organization or religion. They never mentioned, and I never asked, if any governing organizations existed among them.

I had a very difficult time comprehending and believing in these explanations at that time.

It was happening, and I had to accept it as fact—in spite of my skepticism. I had not yet learned to think outside of accepted knowledge. If it did not fit into my frame of knowledge, it could not exist or was wrong. Well, there was a lot of information coming my way that was outside of my frame of knowledge.

I became reclusive and self-absorbed. I stopped talking to my Japanese friends and also to some of my other associates at the university. The only time I talked to people was when I or someone else needed something. I was smoking constantly. I drank coffee while I was awake and did not sleep much. After a while, I quit attending classes. I turned myself over to this bizarre situation. Deep down in my mind, I sensed that there was something I had to find—but what and where? There was an internal feeling in me that I had to correct something, but I did not have the slightest idea what it was in regard to. I did not know why I had this sensation.

I do not remember if I liked it or not that they were around me. When I asked them why they were bothering me, there was no answer.

I think my roommate realized that something was amiss. The situation between us was not the same as it had been. My roommate had ordered a model airplane, which was powered by lighter fluid and flew in a circle at the end of a wire that someone holds. He asked me to go to the hobby shop and pick it up for him. He may have been concerned that I was spending too much time in the room. I was absorbed in thinking of the past and in the communication process, so I did not want to go. But he continued to ask me for over an hour. Finally, I agreed and went and picked it up. I ended up being very glad I'd gone, because during the subway ride the voices left me alone. I stopped thinking about the situation. I picked up the package from the store and brought it back to him at the dormitory. I can still remember him, his nephew, and me flying this plane at his parents' house in the spring during Easter vacation.

These spirits had an agenda that I was not aware of at that time. Today I know what it was about, and my feelings are much different about them because of this. They were trying to make me feel comfortable with them being around me. This was not easy for me by any means. I think they wanted me to have confidence in them, and they also wanted to reduce my fear of them.

I had never known anyone who communicated with spirits, and I felt at a loss with this phenomenon. The closest thing to spirit communication I'd ever heard of was from our neighbors in Hungary. That family told us that a cabinet door in their bedroom kept opening, regardless of what they did with it, short of nailing it. The cabinet belonged to the man's father. They attributed the incident to his father's restless spirit, and the family prayed for him to move on. It did not happen again after the completion of the family praying for him. Maybe he'd decided to move on and was just saying a last good-bye to the family.

Another problem I had with this was that I'd always considered the human spirit to be inferior to us as human beings. I could not initiate communication with spirits, but apparently they could start and continue it. Suddenly, the spirits appeared to be superior to us human beings. I felt bad about this misconception. The thought of their superiority also scared me.

I was skeptical of the whole thing. I also did not want to tell anyone, because I didn't feel comfortable talking about it and felt it was nobody's business. I was a very private person. I learned early in life that some people are jealous of others' successes and lifestyles. One had to trust people selectively with the things he or she did in life.

I'd believed that the knowledge in my brain was secret. The invasion of my mind by these spirits caused me considerable anxiety for several months. I didn't like sharing my intimate life with anybody, not even a spirit. But in this case, I had no choice. All my failures and successes with sex—and everything else—were open to them. I had to learn to accept myself the way I was, and they knew it.

This was the most interesting and the most taxing time of my life. This type of communication can scare the heck out of you. There are probably people who'd welcome it and enjoy the attention these unseen able beings give, but I was not one of those people at that time.

It definitely depends on the mental attitude of a person. This communication challenges the mental stability of a person.

The spirit also said to me, "People are talking about you." After hearing this statement, I had difficulty for several days. When I would look at people conversing and the voice said, "People are talking about you," I assumed the people I was looking at were talking about me. This happened about fifteen times during the course of several days. It became ridiculous. I finally asked the spirits, "Why do you say everybody is talking about me?"

The spirits said, "We did not say everybody is talking about you. We said people are talking about you, but not the people you were looking at." All my friends and acquaintances were probably wondering what had happened to me; that was what the spirits were likely referring to. I just had a hard time comprehending it. After this clarification, the spirits stopped saying that people were talking about me.

I slowly realized that what the spirit voices said might not have anything to do with what I was looking at unless it was strictly specified that it did. I had to learn to discipline my thinking. They were teaching me something that I desperately needed to know, but I just did not know what it was or how to learn it.

There were a few more things they wanted me to do. These requests led to incidents that reshaped my thinking about the spiritual world and its relationship to the human race.

The spirits told me to go down to the corner of Broadway and 110th Street. They said somebody would be waiting for me and would come over and talk to me. I was very skeptical about this, but I went.

When I arrived, people were going every which way. No one seemed to pay any attention to me. Nobody came over to me and said, "Hey, I am glad you came." I waited for around fifteen minutes before deciding I was going to leave. Just then, the voice said, "Ha, ha, ha! You believe in everything you hear." I did not really trust the voices, but I tested them. I had no idea what they were trying to do.

For example, I liked to drink orange juice, but for about a week orange juice tasted very bitter to me. *What is wrong with this orange juice?* I thought. The question was rhetorical, but the spirits answered it. They told me that the orange juice I was drinking was spiked with some drug, which gave it a bitter taste. They said the CIA was putting drugs in the orange juice, and that an employee of the CIA was under orders to do this to certain people. This seemed really farfetched. It was a possibility, but highly unlikely. *Why would anybody do that to me anyway? I could not be that important to anyone?* I thought.

The spirits said, "Go drink orange juice from some other places and compare their taste." So I did. I walked down to 42nd Street, and on the way down I drank orange juice at five or six different places. *They all taste about the same to me,* I thought to myself.

The spirits responded, "It is virtually impossible that all the orange juices are spiked for your benefit. Isn't it?"

Yes, it does, I thought to myself. Logic must prevail without fear. It appeared to me that, whatever the spirits' aim was, they wanted my mind to work correctly. Since they did not tell me why they sometimes misled me, I only could guess at their motivations. In my estimation, these spirits wanted to see how I'd react to the misleading information. I did not become angry or disappointed with them. What I adopted from this was that I became more skeptical about all information that came to my mind. I scrutinized my thoughts more for accuracy. They may have known what was in my mind, but they didn't know how I would respond to information when it resurfaced. I think they had to verify my responses to past incidents for themselves. If any correction were needed, they would help me correct it.

I did not lose my reasoning process. The spirits did not seem to want that either. In fact, I had a feeling that they were pushing me to correctly differentiate between imagination, reality, wishful thinking, things I needed to know, and things I needed to do. They also wanted me to be able to differentiate between my thinking and their communication. They did not explain it to me, but I sensed the difference and I never confused the two.

I did not become obsessed with any ideas, any bodily needs, or any objects. I think they were immunizing me to adverse incidents and thoughts. I could not tell whether these communicators were friends or foes at this time. It became obvious as time went on that they were friends. The communication with the spirit world was extremely valuable to me. It opened my mind to a world that I knew very little about and where I may eventually spend a long time in. After all, the human race and the earth will one day be "Once upon a time there was …"

Chapter 5

The River

In the spring, the spirits asked me to walk down to the Hudson River. They did not specify why they wanted me to go. I was deathly afraid of going to the Hudson River; I think I was afraid I would fall into it. The spirits asked me to slowly approach it, one hundred yards at a time, and come back and do it about two times a day

It took me several weeks of conscience effort to be able to go to the Hudson River. Finally I stood on the bank, and the fear of the river was gone. The fear may have had to do with an incident that occurred when I was about thirteen years old. I was bathing at a dammed up brook with a group of boys. One of the older boys pushed me under the water for a short time. I was fighting for air; I felt like I was suffocating. I did swallow some water and probably got some in my lungs, because I was coughing up water after I surfaced. To add insult to injury, he laughed at me. My fear of the river may have had this origin, but it wasn't apparent to my conscious mind. The fear had to be eliminated.

I constantly had the feeling that I had to correct something. Therefore, I randomly rehashed incidents that happened to me or around me. The selection of specific incidents was random and accidental; they just popped into my head, probably depending on how I felt about it. Judging it from hindsight, the selection may have been directed by the spirits. Most of the incidents recorded in my brain had negative connotations, even if the outcome of it was good. I had to mentally revisit everything, from how I learned to wipe my buttock to how I learned to have sex with girls—and everything between.

I noticed that the intensity of associated negative feelings was 70–80 percent stronger than that of the pleasant feelings, regardless of the end results of the incidents. This was causing a considerable emotional conflict. There was a lot of work to be done to correct this. It appeared to me that the spirits wanted all incidents in my life to be as matter-of-facts. The incidents from my past should not make me too exited or too depressed. Therefore, I said to myself, *This is who I am. I cannot change the past. I will be cheerful about my life.* This was easier said than done.

Chapter 6

Fire in the House

One of the memories I examined occurred when I still lived at home. Soldiers had been stationed in the forest near our village when the war was moving through our area. They'd buried military hardware and ammunition in the ground, hoping to come back to get them after the war. I searched the area and found a device that was part of some food-heating equipment for the army. I remember seeing a similar piece of equipment being used by the soldiers. It was screwed into a container that air could be pumped into. The air forced lighter fluid up through small holes. When it was lit, after it warmed up, the heat gasified the fuel and then it came out as vapor.

I decided to build the missing parts. I did this inside our house in the storage room. I drilled a hole in the top cover of a paint can, screwed the device into the hole, and attached a metal tube to the bottom with a rubber tube to be able to bring the fuel up. I put a bicycle tire valve into the side of the can to allow me to pump air into the container. It was done. I filled the gallon-sized can with about four inches of gasoline, put a tight-fitting lead on, pumped some air into it, and lit it up.

It worked perfectly ... for a few minutes—and then disaster struck. As the top of the paint can warmed up, the dry paint loosened from around the can cover and the top popped open.

The fumes from the can caught on fire. I tried to push the top back onto the can with my foot, but I knocked the can over instead. The burning fuel started running toward combustible materials. I was very scared. Suddenly, my father's teaching on how to put fire out came into my head: cut the air supply to the fire and suffocate it. The attic stairs were right next to me. I ran up and closed the door to reduce drafts. I then ran to the kitchen and got two five-gallon cans of water and poured them around the fire to make the surroundings wet so they wouldn't burn as easily. We always had three five-gallon cans of water in the kitchen, because we had a fifty-feet-deep well that we had to pull water up from. My mother asked me what happened. I don't think I answered her. She saw the fire and ran to get my father, who was with the bees in the backyard. I picked up a bunch of old clothing that we used to cover our beehives in the winter to protect them from frost and throw them on the fire to try to cut the air supply to it. The flames went out; nothing started to burn. My father came in a minute after I put the fire out and asked me what had happened. I told him what I'd been doing and what had happened. He said, "You did a good job putting the fire out and not panicking." To my surprise, he actually complemented me.

I was happy that my father had lectured us about fire prevention. He said, "When you do something like this again, tell me about it and do it outside. Before you do anything, find out if you are doing the right thing and you are doing everything right."

Chapter 7

Bird's Nest

Once I took our family's cows to a valley to eat grass. There was a small patch of trees there, and I noticed that there was a bird nest up in one of the trees. Of course, I had to go up and see what was in it. The tree was actually twisted together from three different trees. Someone, years before, had twisted three saplings of different trees together. Each was about six inches in diameter now. I reached the nest and looked into it, but it was empty. I accidently placed my foot on a dead branch as I was coming down, and it broke under my weight. My hand slipped off the branch I was holding, and my right wrist got caught between the twist on two of the three trees. A piece of dry, broken branch was sticking out from one of the trees and was digging into my thumb area. I found myself in an awkward position, with my back to the tree, hanging by my right hand.

There was nobody around whom I could call for help. The valley was about three miles from the nearest house. People rarely came to this part of the field this time of the year. I was scared stiff. I suddenly realized that I could die there, hanging by my hand, if nobody found me. I had an excruciating pain in my arm. I realized that I had to come up with a solution—and come up with it fast. I used my left hand to try to grab a branch, which was about ten inches out of my reach. *I have to get out of here*, I thought, *and fast, because I am losing strength by the minute.* My survival instinct kicked in. I managed to put my legs behind me around the tree, pushing and pulling myself up with my hanging arm. I was then able to grab a nearby branch. I pulled myself up about a foot, and I was able to free my right hand. I climbed off the tree slowly and very carefully. It was a great relief when my foot finally touched the ground. I never told anyone that I'd gotten stuck on a tree because I wanted to look into a bird nest. This experience left me with an enormous fear of climbing trees. The fear was so intense that when I later tried to climb another tree, I could go only halfway up and had a difficult time coming back down. I would go back to those woods periodically and look at the twisted trees where I got stuck.

Chapter 8

Grain Transportation

Hungary was governed by a semisocialistic political system. The government required that a certain amount of the farm products—such as wheat, rye, potatoes, lard, eggs, and honey—from each farmer had to be sold to the state at a preset price. There was a storage location in each village for the collected goods. When the collection was completed, the collected products were transferred to railroad cars and transported to cities, where they were sold in various forms to the public.

The grain transfer was done by people with horse-pulled wagons. They were paid according to the weight carried. We had horses, which my older brother used to do some of the transportation. He used to do all the farmwork, relying on the help of other people when it was necessary. When some work had to be done in timely fashion, the farmers would help each other. When he turned twenty-one years old in 1950, he was drafted into the infantry division of the Hungarian armed forces. I, at the age of seventeen, had to take over all the farmwork, including the transportation of grains to the railroad station. I knew how to do everything—in theory. I also had experience, but there were holes in my experience, which almost turned the situation into disaster for us.

I was transporting somewhere between five thousand to ten

thousand pounds of grain with the horses. We had to go down a hill. The hill was a reverse z shape about four hundred yards long. The first part of the hill was not very steep, but the second part was much steeper and the third part was even steeper. At end of the second part was a 90-degree turn. There were also three ways to go. Two of the roads were going uphill, and the third was going downhill.

Another young man and I were holding two four-by-four pieces of wood over the back wheels of the wagon to slow its descent. As we were getting close to the end of the second part of the hill, the wagon started gaining speed; our weight was no longer sufficient to slow down the wagon. It was our weight that counted—not our strength. The wagon could not be stopped. I was trying to guide the horses onto the uphill road, but I was not quick enough. The leash was not in my hand, and by the time I grabbed it, the horses had made the turn. I saw that the wagon was going to crush the horses if I tried to hold them back. In desperation, I hit both horses to make them move faster, as I was standing on the ground. Halfway down the hill, about two hundred yard away, was our neighbor with his wagon and horses. I yelled at him to get out of the way. He saw that our horses were coming down the hill fast and seemed to be out of control. He quickly got his wagon to the left side of the road just as our horses and wagon passed him. My friend and I were temporarily paralyzed watching the horses galloping down the hill.

The road divided in two at the bottom of the hill. One road went straight; the other turned left—the way we were supposed to go to get to the city. Both of the roads became flat shortly after the bottom of the hill. There was a fifteen-feet-high mound between the two roads, and I was hoping they would not crash into it. I was also hoping the horses would take the straight road—the easy way out—but they did not. I could not move until the horses made the left turn and were out of sight. I ran as fast as I could to catch up with them. When I got to the bottom of the hill, I saw the horses still pulling the wagon. I ran over to them and stopped them. I hugged them both and gave them each a kiss on the neck. It is hard to explain the happiness I felt. I then saw that the outer leg of each horse was outside of one of the ropes they pulled the wagon with. The inside of their leg above the knee for about a foot was rubbed bloody on both horses. It was an enormous effort by the two horses to guide the wagon as it was rushing downhill. They could not stop it, but they were able to run with it and guide it. It was a miracle that they did not crash. I placed their legs back correctly around the rope.

I drove the grain to the railroad station to unload it and then went to see my father in the hospital. He was in the hospital with bronchial asthma. The first thing out of his mouth was, "What happened?" He could tell something was wrong by the look on my face. I told him that I'd taken the grain to the railroad station, but I did not tell him about the mistake I'd made. He did not ask me about it again. I still do not know if someone told him about the incident. I put some creosote on the legs of the horses to prevent infection, and they healed without any scars. My father was in the hospital for a month, so I don't think he ever noticed. But, then again, he would not have told me if he had anyway. I never told him what happened. We never talked about it.

The feeling that I had to correct something in my past was very intense, and yet I could not figure out what it was. I could not pinpoint anything, because I'd done many things and a lot of them were wrong. I decided to continue examining my life in more detail to see I could find anything to correct.

Chapter 9

1933–1942

I was born on January 17, 1933, in Nagymizdo, Hungary. It was a small farming village about a mile long and contained about ninety houses. There was a grocery store, a schoolhouse, a church that was used for services once a month, and a mill used to produce flours, which also serviced four other villages.

My father, George Papp, was nineteen and my mother, Maria Bedics, was seventeen when they got married. My father worked as an orderly in a hospital in Budapest for two years and saved enough money to buy a house in the village.

My parents had three other children. The oldest one was a girl Margit, born in 1924. She died from pneumonia when she was four years old. My older brother Imre was born on April 4, 1929. My younger brother Jozsef was born on January 22, 1944.

My father was a beekeeper and a farmer. Our house was on a side street of the village where I was born. He did not like the location of the house and built a new house at the end of the village on the main highway. He sold the old house with the agreement that he could keep some of his beehives on their property permanently. I think he gave the new owner some honey every year.

The mill was about one hundred yards from our new house. There were about fifty acres of public land across the street from our house. Since it was public land, the people from the village used to take dirt from it to use at their homes. About half of this land was full of small ponds. There were many frogs in the ponds; in the summertime, they made a lot of noise in the evening until about eleven o'clock, when they would suddenly all stop croaking. The people in the village called it the frog castle. The other half of the land had a soccer field on it. This land and several thousand acres of forest and grassland were owned by shareholders from the village.

Some of the land was also used by the people from the village for their pigs. There was a pig herder who took care of the pigs from sun up to sun down every day. He collected the pigs in the morning from one end of the village to the other and drove them all day on the public land. He let them go home in the evening. Interestingly, each pig knew where it lived. They were not as dumb as people made them out to be.

I do not remember much of my early years. My father and mother told me that I didn't like the new house at all. I kept telling them for several months after we moved into the new house that I wanted to go home. Each house was located on about a four-acre lot, and we had a large collection of beehives at the new house too. I had to share a room with my older brother in both houses.

My father had about ten acres of land where we grew crops: corn, wheat, rye, oats, potatoes, beets, cabbages, and various other vegetables. We had many chickens, geese, pigeons, a few pigs, and several cows. We had four acres of land for grapes and used to produce about two thousand liter of wine a year, depending on the weather. We had several acres of land spread around in different location in the village. My father used to rent another four acres of land next to our house, because our chickens and geese used to damage the crops that grew on that land; that way they would be damaging our crops, which was not a problem. If the damage was done to some other person's crops, then a group of men from the village would evaluate the damage and the person had to be compensated for the damage, either with crops or money. My father tried to avoid the animals causing problems by leasing the land.

The school was about one kilometer from my home, at the other end of the village. The school taught up to only sixth grade. There were ten children in my class about twenty-five in the entire school. We were all friends, since the entire village was small and we all used to play together. We went to school for only four hours a day, from eight in the morning to noon. We had one teacher, and she was in charge of teaching everything. Sometimes she would ask some of us to practice subjects that we were not good at in the afternoon at her house.

The earliest memory I have that is tied to a time sequence is the day when the Second World War broke out. I was six years old. I was with a group of people returning home from church on a Sunday in 1939. Someone said, "Did you guys hear? The war broke out." I really did not know what that meant to me or to us until a few years later.

Several people who were about my father's age were drafted into the army. My father was not drafted, because he had lung asthma and was deemed medically not fit. Some people openly complained about that.

I was about six or seven years old when we slaughtered a fattened pig. This usually was a family event. Close relatives were invited to help with the butchering. My uncle put his coat on the bed in a way that made the coins fall out of his pocket. I found the coins, and the next day I gave them to my father. The money did not mean anything to me. He asked me, "Where did you get the money?" I told him I found the coins on the bed. I don't remember whether my father asked my uncle if he'd lost any money or if my uncle came and asked if we'd found any money. I think my parents had enough sense to know where the money came from. My mother told me that my uncle was blaming his wife for taking the money. This made me feel bad. Somehow it never occurred to me that the money fell out from someone's coat pocket. I did not have enough sense to realize that it was not lost money.

My father used to tell us, "If you find something, someone lost it and probably will be looking for it. Be ready to return it to the person." My father was a very honest man. He did not take anybody's property and would not let anyone take his. He would sell it or give it away.

Most people in our region were respectful of others' properties and took care of them. The people in the village had respect for each other and for private property, and they usually helped others in need.

The Second World War changed some of these things. The people became affiliated with different political parties and started to mistrust each other. There was an old man in the village who handled death certification; he belonged to the Communist Party. He advocated that if Communism came, all hills would be eliminated. I don't think he knew what Communism was about. He confused the concept of "same level" in the social system with ground level. The younger people used to make fun of his believe system—of course, not in his presence. Certain items became scarce, and some select groups of people helped each other while withholding help from other people.

Chapter 10

1942–1945

The war was raging on. Stories about the war filled newspapers and magazines. We usually bought two weekly magazines that reported about the war: a Hungarian magazine called *Runner* and a German magazine called *Signal*.

Germany occupied Hungary in the early part of 1943. We were going to the market in a nearby city one Monday morning, and the German invading forces—cars, trucks, armored cars—were coming in on the highway at high speed all day long. They were driving down the middle of the road; very few people could use the road that day.

Several members of the German armed forces were stationed in our village for about two months. I remember they were collecting supplies, such as hay, corn, and oat for the German army.

One German general was stationed in a house about one hundred yards from our home. There was an interpreter with him who barely spoke Hungarian. My mother had to go over to see him, because my father was not well. He yelled in German at my mother so loudly that we could hear him from where we stood outside of our house. She said later that she did not know what he was yelling about. My mother did not understand a word of German. The Germans used intimidation on everyone. An incident occurred involving our cows pulling a wagon. We

THE FORGOTTEN CONTRACT 41

used to drive on the left side of the road like the British. When the Germans came, we had to switch to the right side. The cows were trained to go on the left side of the road with the wagons without any help. Once, our cows with the wagon ran in front of an oncoming German car. The driver jumped out of the car and began screaming at my father in German. My father kept saying to the driver, "Tell the cows ... Tell the cows." We did not know what he was screaming about. I guess that is how some people behave when they believe they are superior to everybody. The Germans moved on from our village a few weeks later. It took us about a year to retrain the cows to go on the right side of the road without any assistance.

We used to watch British and US planes flying high over the area heading to bomb airports, railroad stations, and military targets in Hungary. One time one of the bombers must have been hit, because it fell back from the formation, dropped its bombs, and turned back. The bombs exploded harmlessly in the meadow.

Another time, we were picking grapes and suddenly all kinds of thing were falling from the sky: machine guns, jackets, chocolates, and helmets. We did not see the airplane that dropped them; they were way too high, and the air was too hazy. We only heard their noise.

Yet another time, a group of bombers was flying back toward England when suddenly one of the bombers fell back from the formation and began losing altitude. It started to circle. One after another yellow parachute appeared high up in the air—nine of them in all. The airplane was still circling and losing altitude rapidly. We thought the pilot wanted to land it, but then another chute appeared. He apparently aimed the plane at the railroad tracks. The bomber broke into thousands of pieces as it hit the tracks. We rode there on bicycles. The German and the Hungarian army were cordoning off the area when we arrived. The wreckage was about three hundred yards in diameter. We did not see any of the crew from the airplane.

I saw several air battles between fighter planes. One of the US or British fighter planes was trailing smoke. It was only a few thousand feet up in the air. The pilot jumped out of it, and the plane crashed. Two of the other fighter planes looked like they were trying to hook onto his chute but were unsuccessful. The pilot landed, and the two fighters left. I was witnessing a dogfight between the German and Hungarian fighter planes and the US twin-engine, double-bodied fighter planes. They were the masters of the sky. The planes were as good as the pilots who flew them. The US planes would force the German and the Hungarian fighters to ground level. The planes were barely above the trees at some point. The US plane was shooting so rapidly that hundreds of the expended shells were falling around us. We ran into the forest to avoid being hit by the falling shells. We could see the tracer bullets going in the air. Suddenly, one of the German or Hungarian fighters was trailing smoke and was going down. Some of us kids from the village had front row seats to a few great air battles.

Three regiments of Hungarian soldiers came into the village in the early fall of 1943. They were called the antitank unit, but they had no cannons, only rifles. They were spread all over the village in different houses, depending on space availability. Some of the soldiers took up residency in the schoolhouse until the end of March 1945, and we were not able to attend school while they were there. A colonel was in charge of the three units. A lieutenant was in charge of each regiment. There were three other second lieutenants and several master sergeants with the three regiments. They had cooking facilities set up at the backyard of a bar, which had a large outside area for dancing. The soldiers had to go there three times a day to eat.

The colonel and one of the lieutenants lived in our house. My mother and an army cook, who used to be an assistant chef in a hotel, used to cook for them. All officers, from master sergeants on up, had some private homes cooking for them in the village. One day in the spring of 1944, I was asked by the lieutenant who lived in our house to take some papers to a soldier who was staying in the school. They had makeshift mattresses made out of straw and blankets to sleep on. I rolled all over the mattresses for about half an hour before returning home. About a week later, my father noticed that I was scratching myself on the side. He asked me, "Why are you scratching yourself?"

"It is very itchy," I said.

He said, "Let me look at it."

He looked at my side and then at my pants. He found some lice. We did not allow bed bugs in the house, let alone lice. He knew that I had been at the school where the soldiers were staying and assumed I picked this up there. He talked to the colonel about it. Well, after that, all the problem showed up. The soldiers in the school and their bed facilities were checked for lice. Two of them had lice, and they were punished. Every soldier from the three units had to come to our front yard and watch the punishment of these two fellows. I watched it too.

Two soldiers tied together the hands of each victim behind their back. Using a long rope thrown over a wooden beam in the hay barn, they were hoisted up so their feet were about a foot from the ground. They hung there for between fifteen to thirty minutes. I do not remember the time exactly, but I remember both of them passed out. After that they lowered them, and two buckets of cold water were poured on their heads and bodies. Their uniforms and the straw used for their beds were burned. They had to report for lice inspections for weekly for a few months.

My father used to buy pigs and calves and barrels of good-grade wine for the officers. There were usually two medium-sized barrels of wine for the officers in our storage room. About twice a month, they gave some wine to the soldiers too. The pigs and calves were slaughtered, and we and the officers lived well in spite of government restrictions on food items—until Miklos Horthy, the president of Hungary, resigned and Ference Szálasi, a Nazi, took over the presidency.

All the people who were Nazis wore an armband indicating that they were members of the Nazi Party. The Nazis were supposed to be taking over the running of the villages for only a few weeks. There was a rumor that if the Germans had even one square mile of territory left, they would still win the war. This was an utmost stupidity to believe, but one could not say that.

Our neighbor's adopted son suddenly became a Nazi Party member and came over to tell the colonel that he and a master sergeant in the army, who was also a member of the Nazi party, were now in charge of all the military in the village. There were also other Nazis from a nearby city. They were arrogant and walked around like the most important people in the land.

The Nazis were setting up a court-martial and drumming up false charges against the officers and my father because of the wine and meat purchasing. I think it was strictly based on jealousy by the Nazi Party members. The day for the court-martial was set, but it was abandoned a day later because the Soviet military forces were coming too fast.

The Soviet military was believed to be only a few weeks away from our area in March of 1945, but this was an underestimation. We could hear the sound of the Soviet artillery and the rocket launchers booming day and night. The Soviet air force was flying reconnaissance missions as well as attacking military targets in the area. Sometimes they were shooting around civilians too, perhaps to scare people.

All the Hungarian soldiers and officers in the village changed into civilian clothes. A large percentage of them disappeared into the forests around the village. Some of them blended in with the village people for some time and then went home. The military uniforms were hidden from the invading forces by the people in the village. Most of their guns were stored in the firehouse. We buried the uniforms of the two officers who'd lived in our house, along with my father's trumpet, in the shack where the firewood was kept.

Chapter 11

The War Comes to the Village

The front of the war was passing over us on the early part of April 1945. A major highway was about three kilometers away from us. We lived on the edge of the village near a forest in the second house on a secondary highway. We have noticed a few *Panzerfaust* (antitank weapon) firing positions around the intersection of the two highways several weeks before. The Panzerfaust were fired at a tank from an L-shaped hole in the ground. There was about a ten- to fifteen-feet-long flame that would come out the opposite end of the Panzerfaust when it was fired; the L-shaped hole was to turn the flame 90 degrees so it did not burn the gunner.

We had three Hungarian soldiers dressed in civilian clothes with us on the fourth of April. The trees had no leaves on them yet, as it was early spring, and we could see around four to five kilometers away. We could hear and see that many of the Soviet tanks and trucks had been moving fast on the road all morning. We saw the flames of several Panzerfaust shots the Germans had made at the tanks. They must have missed or just disabled some tanks, if any, because none of the tanks seemed to be on fire. About noon, a Russian T-34 tank and a small armored car came slowly up the hill about four hundred meters from our house. They waited for about half hour on the top of the hill at the edge of the forest and then came to our house very slowly. Three soldiers came out of the armored car and one came from the tank; they were looking for Germans. We told them with all kinds of words and hand signal that there were no Germans anywhere. They were offering cigarettes to the men and smoked some themselves. After about an hour, they turned around and went back the way they'd come.

That night, my brother and I went to sleep late in the hay in the stable. The next morning, my father rushed into the stable with a lot of noise and a loud voice said, "*Get up! The Russian are here!* Get dressed and come inside. We have to get out of the house and go to your grandparents' house." He ran back inside the house. I did not really know what was going on. We got dressed quickly and went outside. To our surprise, the entire yard was full of horses and wagons. There must have been fifty horses eating hay from about twenty wagons and from the ground. My brother and I hadn't woken up when all these horses and wagons moved onto our yard, and they hadn't come into the stable. We entered the house. A radio operator sat in the hallway at a table working with his communication system. There was a large window between the kitchen and the hallway and another between the front yard and the hallway. The operator could look into the kitchen and out to the yard. We went into the kitchen, and there were about ten to fifteen soldiers drinking our wine. Some were probably quit drunk by then. My brother and I went over to my father; he was sitting on the side of the bed where my mother was. She was trembling and had a horrified look on her face. My brother and my father helped my mother get out of bed. My father picked up my fifteen-month-old brother, and all five of us started toward the kitchen door. The soldiers in the kitchen got up and seemed to be asking where my mother was going. At this point, the radio operator came into the kitchen and helped my father and my brother assist my mother out of the house. He kept repeating "Russian doctor" and said several other sentences.

After the radio operator's words, which we did not understood, the others seemed to be satisfied and got out of the way and sat down. The radio operator came with us to the front yard and pulled the horses heads away so we could go by them. He came out to the street with us and was urging us by waving both of his hands in the air to get fast away from there. He seemed to be very happy that we were going away. I am sure the other soldiers were drunk, and they were planning to rape my mother. The Russian radio operator knew exactly what their plan was. He was a decent man and knew what could possibly happen; that is why he wanted us out of the house. Looking back now, and knowing my father, I think we avoided a bloodbath. My father mentioned to us later that the radio operator had been signaling him with his hand to come out and go away. I don't know how long it took my father to decide that we would leave the house.

I've thought about this radio operator many times over the years. He may have saved our lives. I hope he had a good life. He probably is no longer alive, but I wish him good luck wherever he is.

We were going to my grandparents' house. They had a cellar where they stored vegetables for the winter. On the way, we were going to pass by my uncle Tony's house, who lived about two hundred yards from us. As we were nearing his house, one of us noticed that a Russian soldier was coming after us on a bicycle with a submachine gun flung over his shoulder.

My father said, "What the heck does he want now? Let's go into Tony's house," and that we did in a hurry. The soldier arrived at the front yard, put the bicycle down, came inside, and asked my father and my uncle to come out of the house. He pulled their boots off, put them on the handlebar of the bicycle, and went back to our house. My father was barefooted as we continued on to my grandparents' house, but we arrived without any other incident. We stayed in the cellar with my grandparents and some neighbors. A Russian soldier came down into the cellar at about one in the afternoon. He spoke some Hungarian and played with my one-year-old brother and sang to him for about twenty minutes and then left.

The Russian soldiers occupied the entire village. Three Russian officers were staying at my other uncle's house, which was about three hundred yards from my grandparents' house. These officers said that the soldiers were permitted to do anything in a freshly entered area for twenty-four hours. Drinking, raping, and pillaging were on the schedule. The officers would not stop them. After twenty-four hours it will be a different story. My uncle's wife made some Hungarian food for the officers: chicken in sour cream sauce with home-style egg noodles. She told us that two of the officers were eating with fork and knife while the third officer was just looking at them. When the two officers finished eating, they left the room. At that time, the third officer mixed some of the egg noodles with the chicken in the sour cream sauce and began eating by scooping the chicken and the noodles with his hand and putting it into his mouth. Apparently the two officers who left the room could not stand the eating habits of the third one.

Later that afternoon, I, my brother, two of my cousins, and about three other kids from the village went to my house to see what was going on. When we were about fifty feet from the house, we heard several short submachine gun bursts. They were shooting with the submachine guns at the chickens and the pigeons. Two days later, the soldiers moved on—taking with them about ten horses from the village—and we went home.

We found a horrible site. The entire front yard was full of hay and horse manure. The bedroom walls were sprinkled with chicken blood, and chicken feathers were stuck to the blood. They decorated the pictures on the walls with chicken intestines. They ransacked the house and found the magazines we collected, the *Runner* and the *Signal*. They tore most of them into pieces and dispersed them all over the bedroom and the kitchen.

The Russian soldiers used their bayonets to look for buried valuables. They found the uniforms and tore them and urinate on them and also in several places in the bedroom. They stomped on the trumpet so much and so hard that air could hardly be blown through it. They also destroyed my father's harmonica.

There was a fourteen-year-old girl who was raped by about six Russian soldiers. Several other women were also raped, including the young wife of a math teacher in the next village. She was a very nice woman in her early thirties. As far as I heard, she was raped by ten Russian soldiers. She was mentally and physically hurt. Her hands were always shaking to varying degrees even four years after the war. I do not know whether she ever recovered from the trauma. As time went on, people pushed aside thoughts of the war and rarely talked about it, but the hatred of the Russian soldiers stayed with them.

The hatred of the Germans by the Russians was manifested in a very gruesome way. I did not see this, but I heard about it from some people from our village who were going to see their relatives in the next village immediately after the Russian army moved out. There was a wounded German soldier on the top of the hill by the road, and a Russian soldier was guarding him. An army utensil, one end is a fork and the other is a spoon, was shoved into his throat in a way that the spoon side was down his throat and the fork part was by his upper teeth. He was moaning and groaning. Some people went over to help him, but the Russian guard chased them away. The guard stayed there until he died; after that, he left. The people from the next village buried him in their cemetery. This soldier was probably one of the ones who fired the Panzerfausts at the Russian tanks and had been wounded by the Russians as he was trying to get away.

About two weeks later, two Russian soldiers came and brought a pair of boots. The boots looked like they were my father's boots; they wanted to trade them for wine. My father thought they would take the wine anyway, so he gave them wine and they left the boots. A day later, my father noticed that two Russian soldiers were coming across the field. My father said, "Those are the same guys who were here yesterday. They are coming for more wine or the boots or both.

Lock all the doors, and let's get out of here." When they saw us leaving, the soldiers started to run toward us. We did not have a chance to get out of the front gate.

A new house was being built about fifty yards from our house. About ten to fifteen of the people who worked there must have seen the soldiers were coming. They all came running up to our house, including my uncle Joseph, and were there by the time soldiers arrived.

One of soldiers was large, about six and a half feet tall, and had a pistol that was stuck in his belt at his belly area. The other one was shorter, about five and a half feet tall, and had as submachine gun in his hands. He did the talking; the other one was about ten feet away from him. The group of villagers was about fifteen feet away from my father and the soldier, who was pointing the submachine gun at my father's belly. They were demanding more wine. When my father refused to give them some, they wanted the boots back. Maybe they wanted everything—we just did not understand them well. My father had had enough of these freeloaders, as he called them later on. He grabbed the submachine gun in the soldier's hand, and the struggle was on for the gun. My father was fighting for his life and his family. The Russian was fighting for his honor and maybe for his life. The other soldier was pulling the pistol out of his belt and was in the process of lifting it up when my uncle, who was about five feet four inches tall, yelled and jumped on the tall soldier and grabbed his head from the front and the back. The Russian shook himself loose from my uncle's grip and ran outside the gate. He was trying to aim his pistol at my father, but by then my father had the submachine gun in his hands and was aiming at the Russians. My father had very strong hands. He was never in the army, but he sure knew how to hold and aim that gun. None of the other people did anything to help my father or my uncle. All of us, with the exception of my father and my uncle, seemed to be paralyzed. These actions took about a minute. When the tall soldier saw that my father had the gun, he gave his pistol to my uncle. The seventy-two bullets in the submachine gun could have filled the Russians full of holes, and they knew it. The two soldiers were terrified and almost on their knees, begging for their guns to be returned to them. They said if they didn't have the guns, they would be killed. What they probably meant was they would be court-martialed. My uncle took the bullets out of the guns and, with my father's approval, gave the guns back to the Russians—but not the bullets. The requirement was that they never come back. The soldiers left running and disappeared over the hills and never looked back. To kill them would not have been a good idea; even if it had been by accident, it would have been a big, big mistake. Interestingly, I don't remember ever asking my father how he felt about that situation. I probably knew how he felt.

The people in the area had great respect for my father. When I had disagreement or argument over something with someone, I was told by the individual that, "You are just the son of George Papp." Well, I was happy to be that.

A few weeks later, hundreds—maybe thousands—of Cossacks on horsebacks were moving along with many horses. They were taking additional horses and substituting fresh horses for the killed and wounded ones. They took several horses from our village.

The front stalled in the Austrian Alps for a couple of weeks, and a large number of Cossacks with thousands of horses were staying in a meadow about ten kilometers from our house. They rounded up the wounded horses and chased them away around the village. I think they were hoping that the village people would look after them or, if the horses died, and the people would bury them. There were about two dozen wounded, abandoned horses wandering around the village. Most of them died of their injuries. We were feeding three of these horses. Two had lung shots and died within two weeks in our backyard. We had to dump these horses in a canyon area that had about fifty fox holes in the side of a hill. The foxes probably eat the horse carcasses. I looked there six months later, and even the bones were gone. One of the horses had a large wound by the front legs on the neck. It looked like an exploding bullet ripped it open. We patched it up and put some creosote on it for disinfection. This horse survived with our proper care, and we adopted it. Other people in the village also took care of some of the wandering horses.

Three week later, a few regiments of Russian soldiers moved into the forest near our house. They were going to use our bedroom for a hospital room for a violent, deranged officer. The room was not clean, and the commander asked why it was that way. My father told them that the Russian soldiers left it in that state. The commander became very angry and said, "No, no, no. The Germans did it … the Germans did it." My father's explanation fell on deaf ears. We were ordered to clean it immediately. When we finished, they brought the deranged officer there and posted an armed guard at the door. He would yell and scream and throw things around. He broke a few pieces of my mother's china. A doctor came every four hours and treated him. They moved him out after four days and left the room empty. A month later, the soldiers moved on.

Chapter 12

The End of the War

I was taking our four cows out to the field to eat grass one afternoon in the early summer of 1945, when I heard gunshots in the distance. The sounds were coming from the valley and were getting closer and closer. I stopped in the field by the road and wondered, *What is happening?* A horse-pulled wagon was coming up the hill with two Russian soldiers in it. One was driving the horses, and the other, an officer, was shooting his rifle into the air and yelling *"Vojna kaput! Vojna kaput!"* I knew these words. The war was over, and they were going from village to village celebrating.

About two months after the end of the war, an announcement was made that all men in the village must report in person to the sheriff's office on a specified Friday. The rumor was that they were selecting people to take with them to Russia to rebuild their country with war prisoners' labor. Some of the younger people disappeared into the forest so they wouldn't be taken. Some of the older people went, but nobody came to talk to them and they returned home in the middle of the day.

Several regiments of Russian soldiers moved into the forest connected to the next village, Katafa, after the war in 1945. They were a few miles from our house. One day, we were planting potatoes in the land next to our house around the end of April 1946. A Russian soldier, a Cossack, came on horseback into the front yard and started to shoot at the pigeons in the air and the chickens in the yard with a submachine gun. He killed one chicken, picked it up, stuffed it in his saddlebag, and left.

A day later, a high-ranked Russian officer drove up in a jeep and wanted to know how many soldiers had come to us the day before, what had been done, and if anybody had been hurt. He apologized for the shooting and the chicken killing. He spoke a few Hungarian words and said, "They will all be prosecuted for such an action." He was slapping the back of his own head and said, "They will be kaput." The officers were trying to keep order among the soldiers.

They probably were looking for social acceptance with their action.

Chapter 13

Neighborly Love

About twenty T-34 tanks and seventy-five trucks with large cannons along with a large number of Russian soldiers settled into the forest about five hundred yards from our house in the summer of 1947. They built barracks from wood and lived there for about a year. They conducted military exercises a few times during their stay. They gave warning not to be in the target area when they were shooting. The projectiles were traveling about twenty kilometers away, and they blew holes about ten feet in diameter and a yard deep in neighboring land. They did not care whose land they were damaging.

The soldiers would sometimes come out to the village to buy wine, pork products, and some vegetables and fruits they wanted to eat. The military food was probably not all that great for them. They were moving out from the forest in the summer of 1948. Nine Russian officers were drinking in the village and bought a barrel of wine. The Russian officers and a few people from the village came over to our house and asked my father to drive them and the barrel of wine over to the barracks. They told my father that they would fill up the wagon with wood, which was part of the barracks, as payment for the service. My father did not want to do it. He had a bad feeling about the whole thing. The conversation about whether to go or not go went on for about half an hour. I butted into the conversation too. I told my father to take them back, because I wanted to go and see the camp. My father eventually agreed and took the barrel of wine and the officers to their camp; my brother and I went along. The camp was mostly empty. There were no guards, and I did not see any other soldiers. My father, my brother, and I never got off the wagon. The officers took the wine and put it away. They ripped boards off the roof and the side of the barracks and put them in our wagon. The sounds of the nails squeaking as they were coming out of the wood could be heard quite far away. This was a scary sound at night. We left for home when no more wood could fit in the wagon. The Russian officers came back with us. There was a surprise waiting for us when we got home: the Hungarian police were at our house. I do not remember seeing any confrontation between the Russian officers and the police. I do not remember what happened to the wood we were bringing back.

The old police force was replaced by an interim police force, comprised mostly of criminal-minded individuals. The policemen used to ride bicycles in pairs as patrols around the villages. These village night watchmen saw these new policemen stealing chickens at night in several villages.

Two of these police officers must have come by, and our neighbor reported something to them. We do not know what transpired between the police and our neighbor. This was the same neighbor who'd been involved in organizing the Nazi court-martials of the Hungarian military officers. My father was arrested. The police charged him with ordering the Russian officers to shoot at the Hungarian police. He was placed in a concentration camp with war criminals and Nazi sympathizers. This charge was ridiculous. The Russian officers did not even have guns with them, and my father did not speak Russian. The entire thing was orchestrated by our neighbor, who probably wanted the wood and paid off the police.

The concentration camp was about forty kilometers from our

home. My mother used to go and visit him twice a week. My brother or I and her brother used to go to the train station and wait for her to arrive and walk home with her. She was afraid of the dark roads but did not like to ride in buses or cars. We had only one horse and could not use it to travel and pick her up.

My mother came home late one night after a visit. Her brother and I went to the train station to walk home with her. We were walking back on the main highway, because it was very dark and the shortcut would not be safe. A tractor from a collective farm, which was pulling an open-top wagon, was coming down the road. I knew he was going to our village, and I flagged him down. I asked him if he would mind if we got on his wagon and if he could drive us home. I talked my mother into getting on the wagon. She did not like the idea, but she did it. The ride was smooth until we arrived at a steep, curvy hill. We used to call this the "death curve," because many accidents had happened there. The driver of the tractor lost control going down the steep hill near our home. The driver was thrown out of his seat by the strong spring action as the tractor passed over a deep gutter on the side of the road and flipped onto its side and a big tree stump hit the driver's seat. It would have killed the driver if he'd stayed in his seat. Fortunately, the rods connecting the wagon to the tractor bent, and the weight of the five large drums of gasoline contained in the wagon prevented it from flipping over. We were all safe in the wagon. My mother was shook up, but we were all able to walk home. The collective farm had to bring help to upright and remove the tractor the next day.

My father spent almost one month in the concentration camp. When his case came to court, the judge laughed at the charges. The Russians were gone, the charges were dropped, and he came home. I felt terrible for him and for recommending we go because I wanted to see the camp. He probably did not make up his mind about going based on my statement, but I felt bad about it anyway.

This was the second time I felt bad about recommending something that almost ended in disaster. They say bad thing comes in triplicate; the third one was not far behind. Only my father's intuition saved his life. I had nothing to do with it.

The interesting thing was that my father did not have any animosity toward our neighbor. They seemed to still talk whenever they had a chance. I never asked my father how he felt about the whole thing. As a family, we did not discuss it. The people in the village held the neighbor responsible. The actual charges were imposed by the police, and no long-term effects came about from this situation. I did feel resentment toward the neighbor, and I had to overcome that by forgiving him for what had taken place.

Chapter 14

Panzerfaust

My father was a volunteer fireman and was also in charge of taking care of the village fire engines. He had the key to the firehouse; therefore, we had free access to the building where the fire engines were kept. I used to help him keep the fire engines clean.

When the Soviet army was close to approaching our village, the three regiments of the Hungarian army that were stationed here discarded their uniforms and dressed in civilian clothes given to them by the people in the village. They left all their guns in the firehouse. The ex-soldiers waited until a few weeks after the front passed over and then they left. There were about six hundred different kinds of guns and rifles and three German Panzerfausts abandoned at the firehouse. While examining all of these, I found a submachine gun that had been used by the Soviet army. I took home a Hungarian carbine and the Soviet submachine gun. My father took home a German Mauser rifle. The guns were still there in the spring and summer of 1948. I was always looking through these guns and was the one who found the three Panzerfausts. They were actually loaded, only the ignition caps were missing. I took one apart. I took off the head, which was designed to penetrate a tank on impact. Inside the pipe, between two half-inch rubber gaskets, were black triangular-shaped pieces of compacted gunpowder, each about the size of half a grain of wheat. I poured the gunpowder into an empty one-gallon paint can and went with it to my grandparents' house. There was a fire in the kitchen stove, and I wanted to test the power of this gunpowder. I'd heard it was very powerful. Therefore, I took three pieces and put them in the fire. These three small pieces blasted the fire apart. It scared me, and I thought, *Do not fool around with it.* I took the can and hid it in my grandfather's barn area. We were all farmers, and there were lots of places to hide a can on a farm. My grandparents had two state wards—one boy, Steven, and a girl, Irene—who were assigned to stay with them until they were eighteen years old. Steven apparently saw where I hid the can. This was on a Thursday afternoon.

On Sunday, a bunch of us spent most of the afternoon playing soccer on the soccer field near our house. At about five in the afternoon, we noticed a boy from the village was coming fast on his bicycle toward us. He kept yelling, "Jeno, run! Your father is coming with the horses, and he is furious." I asked him why. He said, "Your cousin Gene and Steven who lives with your grandparents said you burned them down at the brook with gunpowder, that is why."

"What are you talking about? I did no such a thing," I said. Just then I saw our horses were coming up fast with my father on the coach. He drove all the way out to the soccer field, and when he got right next to me, he screamed, "Why did you do it?"

"Why did I do what?" I asked him.

"Why did you burn your cousin Gene and Steven?"

I said, "I didn't do it. I was here all afternoon, and I do not even know what you are taking about." All the other players came and told him that I had indeed been there all afternoon.

My father simmered down and said, "Go see what happened to them. They are at your grandfather's house."

I went over to my grandfather's house, which was about half a kilometer away.

The two chaps were sitting in the shade under a huge pear tree with three other fellows. They were in bad shape. There were yellow circles the size of silver dollars all over their chests, on their bellies, and on their legs.

I asked them, "What did you guys do?"

Steven said, "We took the gunpowder you hid and went down to the brook. We wanted to burn the powder. We made a fire and poured the powder onto a large, stretched-out newspaper. The two of us picked up the paper and were carrying it to the fire. We were about two meters from the fire when the gunpowder suddenly exploded. The gunpowder burned our bodies, and we jumped into the water."

"You should not have taken it. I hid it because it was way too dangerous," I said. We took them to the doctor on Monday, and the doctor treated their skin with some ointment. They had to use it for about two months. It took a few months for them to recover, but they did without too many scars. They did not want to take responsibility for their actions. It was a typical human response—always thinking things are someone else's fault.

Chapter 15

Horse Rustlers

The state of Hungary required that the owner of every horse and cow had to have a state-issued ownership paper indicating that the animal belonged to such and such person. There was a description, name, age, sex, and the type of the horse or cow on the paper. A new paper was issued every time the animal was sold to another person, indicating the seller's and the purchaser's home address.

This verification system for the ownership of horses and cows broke down after the war, because the Soviet army was taking and leaving horses all over the places. Stolen horses were driven up to fifty miles away and sold under the pretense that the horses were obtained from the Soviet army. This caused an increase in stealing horses and murdering people to take their horses. Stolen cows were butchered, and the meat was sold on the black market. There was a great food shortage after the war, particularly in the cities. In order to protect our livestock from theft, my brother, I, and our dog slept just inside the open stable door so nobody could come in without stumbling over us.

One night, we were suddenly woken by the vicious barking of the dog. He was attacking someone in the yard just outside the stable door. Whoever it was, he was running out of the yard into the cornfield behind our house with the dog in pursuit. We encouraged the dog to chase the intruder. My father appeared from the house within seconds. He knew from the barking of the dog that there was trouble. He was carrying a German Mauser rifle and a handful of ammunitions for it. He fired four or five shots into the air over the cornfield. The next morning, we found a horse from the village in the cornfield eating. Someone had stolen the horse from the village, and he was going to steal our horse too. Apparently, after my father's shots, he let that horse go. My brother went over to the owner of the horse the next morning and asked him to come and pick it up. A month later, my father bought the horse.

My father was very much attuned to the quiet nights. I remember once he woke up because the chickens were making noise. A fox was getting into the chicken coup. I was amazed by his perceptive abilities.

Chapter 16

Murder

A few months later, one Sunday about noon, three people came to us from the village of Sal, which was about four kilometers from us. They were inquiring about a man from their village who was supposed to have arrived back there that past Friday after coming down our way to take a horse wagon to another village to pick up something from his relatives. After he failed to return, the people had checked with his relatives; they said that he never arrived there. The road he was taking passed in front of our house and five other houses. These people wanted to know if anybody saw him going by, but no one had. My father told them that on Friday afternoon, he had been coming home from his doctor on a coach with the horses. On the other side of the valley, just before he entered the downhill forested area, two men ran toward him and tried to stop him. He said he was scared of them and whipped the horses and galloped down the hill. This took place about the same area where the tractor flipped over.

The people who were looking for the lost man asked us if we would go with them and scan the forest and the roadside to search for him. About fifteen of us from the village went, and we took our dog with us. We started from the other side of valley on the top of the hill where the forest started. Within ten minutes, the dog started to bark—it had found the man's body. He'd been shot in the head and dragged into the forest and left under a bush. We could see from the blood trail the way the body had been dragged from the road to its resting place. The police department was notified, but the murder was never solved. The horses were never found.

We assumed that the people who killed him were the same people who had chased after my father. My father said, "They would have killed me if I picked them up." He'd had a premonition about what was going to happen.

Other people reported suspicious characters walking around that area. They were probably looking for horses to steal. The farmers with horses stopped working the fields alone for several months.

Chapter 17

Temper Control Needed

I am not proud of some of the things I did in the past. I was very shy, and yet I had a quick temper during my early teen life. I was easily angered—very flammable, as some people called it. Once I was reading a book in our kitchen, and my mother asked me to do something for her. I do not remember what it was, but I said, "In a minute."

She said to me, "I want you to do it now." I got very angry, tore up the book, and put it into the fire in the stove. My mother said, "You did not have to do that." I went and did the chore for her. Months later, I wished I hadn't done that. It was a good book

I started to work on controlling my temper, because I found it self-destructive. It was very difficult. I did not know how to do it and periodically would fall back into my old routine. My temper could have been detrimental in my life. I was stubborn when I was young, and that trait carried into my adult life. If it hadn't have been for the stubbornness, I don't think I could have succeeded in life.

My cousin Gene and I used to fistfight a lot, usually two or three times a week. We both had quick tempers and unyielding attitudes. We had dislocated and bruised hands and fingers many times because of the fights. We stopped fighting when we became eighteen years old.

Our family were going to the market in the city one day on a horse wagon. On the way, we saw about two hundred Soviet soldiers were going target shooting practice. About half a mile past them, I saw a magazine on the ground from a Soviet submachine gun. I picked it up. It was full of bullets. Since it could not be returned to anyone, I took it home and hid it in a rabbit cage. I showed it to a boy who was two years younger than me. He stole it a few weeks later, and I got very angry. I picked up a large stick and went to look for him. I planned to beat the living daylight out of him. Fortunately, I did not find him, and the anger tapered off. The amount of anger that I had felt scared me. I could have done very nasty damage to him. I never asked him for the magazine, and I never wanted to be that angry again.

Chapter 18

Growing Up

I was twelve years old when the war finally ended in the summer of 1945. I couldn't attend school in the fall of 1945, because I was too old. I only had a fourth-grade elementary school education.

In 1947, the new government raised the required level of basic education by two years. It was called middle school. All children were required to go to school from age six to fourteen years, after which they could go for four years to a school called Gimnazium and possibly to a university of their choice. The subjects the teachers had to teach also changed. By the time these revisions were in place, I was already fourteen years old and could not go to school anymore. My handwriting was not good, and my sentence writing ability left a lot to be desired. Good penmanship and other similar skills were not taught in the first four grades. I felt grossly undereducated.

We acquired a bicycle after the war. My cousin Gene and I were both fifteen years old. He already knew how to ride a bicycle; I did not. I asked him to teach me how to ride on a bicycle. He explained to me how to do it. I learned to do it on a highway. We went riding up and down for about an hour. He took me onto a narrow path, about a foot wide, that went downhill next to a forest. I was doing great at the beginning, but as the hill got steeper I lost control of the bicycle and ran into an oak tree. The front wheel of the bicycle bent 90 degrees. The right side of my face was badly scrapped as I hit the tree. We straightened the front wheel out, and no one could tell it was ever bent.

I quickly invented a story that I intended to tell my father to explain what happened to my face; I didn't want to tell him the truth. My father asked me what happened to my face when he got home. I told him that I took the cows out to feed on the grass, and one pulled me over a cut down tree stump and that was what scratched my face. He accepted the story. I really did not know why I felt I had to lie. The truth would have been just as good. Was I concerned about a lecture from my father, maybe? Or maybe I did not want to look stupid for running into a tree. I do not know the answer to it.

There was always competition for success and achievement. Individual success was not a public affair. I did not like to talk about what I did, and I did not like people to know about it. People said that life in Hungary was different before the Second World War. After the war, the shortage of food and other items needed by the public and the political changes that occurred altered the behavior of people. We resorted to a life full of cover-ups as opposed to the truth. The government was socialistic and wanted to know how many pigs, cows, and chickens farmers had. How many offspring did these animals have a year? How much wine and grain was produced? We were required to sell to the state a certain portion of these products at a price set by the government. The government wanted to control the life of the farmers. There were constant cover-up stories about everything to try to show that we had less than the actual amount we had. These situations caused people to develop dual behaviors. These could cause emotional conflicts, but most people seemed to function well with it. Providing misinformation was an act of self-preservation, and it became second nature to people. Growing up during these times, it became my second nature too.

I was a very religious young person. I used to go to confession and Communion on the first Friday of every month. I also used to fast often, not eating breakfast, lunch, or dinner, or eating a limited amount. On the first Friday of every month, I would put a needle into one of my finger to draw blood, to share the suffering of Jesus on the cross. I dreamed of becoming a person who would spread Catholicism around the world. I dreamed about martyrdom and how it felt. This may have been a memory from a past life experience, I learned later in life. People in the area thought I was going to be a priest. Yes, I had that in mind. But by around the age of fifteen, I started to notice girls' wider hips, round breasts, higher voices, and a strong desire formed in me to see more. I think the procreation hormones started to take over as the driving force in me. I loved the sight of females. The desire to be with girls or women became so strong in me that it overrode all the fears I'd ever had of the dark or of confrontations with other people. I had the desire to be loved by women. I wanted to feel the tenderness a woman could give to a man. I had a many occasions where I learned the exiting feeling of being near a naked female body. Two merging into one to create a third one is wonderful, but you have to care for the offspring if one comes.

I rode my bicycle many evening to different villages for dates. One time, I was coming home from a date and was about a mile away from our house. I came down one hill and had to push the bicycle up another hill into the dark woods. As I entered the woods, something jumped on me. I was scared stiff for the fraction of a second. The relief from fright came fast, because the thing that jumped on me started to lick my hand. I realized it was our dog. He had been waiting for me so far away from home. How did he know I was going to be coming that way? I will never know. He just knew where to wait. He was a big dog; I was lucky he had not knocked me over. After that, whenever I had been to see that girl and was returning home, I always stopped before I went into the forest and called for the dog. Sometimes he was there, but not always.

I was going to a different village for a date on time, and as I started going down the hill I noticed that there were three gypsies—two of them with axes in the hand—coming onto the road. I stopped the bicycle and came back up the road and took a walking path down the hill. I thought that they would not know that I was bypassing them that way. This path and the main road were separated by about three hundred yards of thick forest. The desire for the relationship overrode all my fears. I did not think of the fact that around one in the morning I would have to come back on the same road. It was very dark, and I had a hard time navigating among the trees and bushes. But it was worth doing it. Sex is the great driving force—but don't overdo it, don't kill for it, and don't hurt other people for it. I did know people who were defeated by fear of darkness or imagination of danger even if there was nothing there to be scared of.

There was an incident when two of my friends from a neighboring village came to our village to hangout and possibly meet some girls. Some of the young men in my village did not like that these two were interested in the village girls. They seemed to be trying to get into a fight with the outsiders. I got involved because the two young men were my friends. I got into an intense verbal argument with one of the village fellows, who seemed to be the instigator. I got angry and punched him in the head with my fist. This young man was the son of the man who took care of the village pigs every day. All five boys from my village started to attack me. The only defense I had was to run away.

I ran into my grandparent's yard. I saw that the two young men from the other village left on their bicycles. I found out the next day that they had not been hurt. After waiting for about half an hour, I came out of the yard and was heading home. Suddenly the five young men from my village began chasing me again. I started to run, but one of them threw a stone after me, which hit me on the head and I collapsed. I tried to stand up, but I was very wobbly. I saw them running away. I staggered like a drunken man in and out of the roadside rain ditch until I made it down to my uncle's house. I went in the yard and sat there for about an hour until the dizziness went away.

The next day, the father of the young man told my father that I'd stabbed his son with a knife. I told my father that was not true and that I had only hit him with my fist, and I showed him where part of the skin had come off my fingers. His father and my father asked us to shake hands and forget the incident. We did just that. We were friends again. Sometimes I gave them wine when they took the pigs for mud baths.

My brother's friend was a shoemaker who worked in the next village. He had to go past our house to get to his work place. He'd bought a motorcycle, and one day he had a flat tire near our house and left the motorcycle with us. I fixed the flat tire and took the motorcycle out for a ride on the highway. The problem was that I was not familiar with traffic rules, and I almost had an accident by passing a bus on the wrong side while it was letting off passengers. I barely made it between the open bus door and the telephone pole. I also used to borrow the motorcycle of a different man and ride it around the villages. One day, he refused to lend it to me anymore. He said I'd left him with a flat tire. I told him I would fix the flat. I think he worried that I might break it, and so he did not let me. I thanked him for the usage and never asked him to lend it to me again.

Chapter 19

Beehive Problem

We had about four acres of farmland and about ten beehives by our home. My father leased four acres of land behind our house to avoid the problem of compensation for crop damage done by our chickens and geese. This way our life was much simpler.

My father wanted to double our number of beehives and was looking for a cabinetmaker to contract out the job to. There was a cabinetmaker in the village. I will call him Jeff, though it is not his real name. My father asked Jeff how much he would charge to make twelve beehives. Whatever price Jeff quoted must have been too high, because my father contracted with Ted, a different cabinetmaker in the city. My father said it cost him less than half of what Jeff wanted to charge him. The beehives were ready three months later.

That year, after the rye harvest in July, the land behind our house was seeded with buckwheat. The ground was pushed down with a heavy roller to crush the lumps of earth to make the land flatter. This process makes harvesting buckwheat with a scythe easier. The buckwheat can be cut down closer to the ground, and the scythe stays sharper for a longer period.

We were sleeping around ten o'clock on a Sunday night in

early August, when someone from the village woke us by banging on the door and shouting that the straw stack in our backyard was on fire. Lots of people came from the village with the fire engine and started to spray water on the part of the house that was threatened by the fire. This part of the house was full of hay and had straw cover on it as its roof. They did not pump water onto the burning straw stack, because it would push too much burning straw up in the air, which could set the house on fire. The dry straw was burning fast, and the fire was making booming sounds like a foghorn. Our next-door neighbor and several other people went up to the straw-covered roof to put out any fires that started on it. Some people asked if there was ammunition hidden in the straw stack that could explode. We assured them that there was none. Some of our relatives who came to help put the fire out were saying that they thought my father had lost his mind, because they had seen him running around barefoot and in long underwear in our relative's backyard. Some people started to accuse our neighbor, saying that they thought he started the fire because of the earlier false accusation he'd made about the Russian soldiers. My father came home about two hours later and put his clothes on. He said he had been checking on someone.

The road that came from the village had a fork in it about two hundred yards from our house. One road went toward the mill and out to the fields. The other road came toward our house and was part of the highway. A man who lived at the mill reported that he saw someone throwing burning matches up in the air. He thought someone was lighting up cigarettes and throwing the matches away. Actually, that someone was the arsonist trying to set the house on fire but the burning matches could not reach the straw part of the house, which was covering the hay storage area; it was too high, about thirty feet. Interestingly, some people who came from the other end of the village to help came in on the backyard path. This was a path that went across every house's backyard and everybody was free to use it. These people had seen

Jeff the carpenter running the other direction on the backyard path. They even said to him, "Where are you running? The fire is at the other end of the village," but they did not get an answer. They told my father about this incident. There was a police patrol in the area that had come over when they saw the fire. They asked my father if he had any idea who started the fire. My father said that he had a fairly good idea who the person was. The policemen said they would report it to the department and someone would come Monday to investigate.

Two detectives came from the city the next day to investigate the arson. They talked with my father and looked at the field behind our house, where they found shoe prints leading away from the house. The detectives went and talked to some of the people who had seen Jeff running down the path. After talking with several people, including the person who saw someone throwing burning matches up in the air, the detectives went over to talk to Jeff the carpenter. He was working on my uncle's house at the time. They talked to him for about two hours and then went with him over to his house, which was next to our relatives' house where my father had been seen in underwear.

The two detectives and Jeff came over to our house later that afternoon. They brought a pair of Jeff's shoes and made him put them on and then asked him to run several different times and different ways on the field behind our house. There was a distinct mark on the bottom of his shoes that was easily matched with the shoe prints that had been left in the freshly compressed field behind the house. Jeff was arrested and charged with arson, and they took him to the police station in the city.

The detectives brought him back in handcuffs two days later. He admitted to my parents that he had lit the fire while he was drunk. He offered compensation to my father to avoid jail time. He promised to build sixteen beehives for my father to avoid jail. The agreement was that he had one year to finish all the hives, otherwise he would be prosecuted. He said many times,

"A horse has four legs and still stumbles. I have only two legs, and I stumbled too." I think he really felt bad about his mistake. He was lucky that he did not set the house on fire. There was never a problem with him afterward. My father had sensed from talking with Jeff a week or two before the fire that he was going to do something nasty. My father was a reasonable man, and he did not want Jeff in prison. I think Jeff had said to my father that he would be sorry for not giving him the contract. Well, he ultimately had the chance to build the beehives.

Chapter 20

Girl with the Truth

When I was about fifteen years old, I wrote a letter to a good-looking girl I liked in the next village. She was a year younger than me, and she had eight years of education. I had less than four years of elementary school education because of having to quit school because of the war.

A group of eight of us, four girls and four boys, were coming home on a horse wagon from a puppet show class in the city. This girl was among us. The first chance she had, she made fun of my letter and me in front of the other people. The letter was full of mistakes, and I had not been able to construct a decent sentence. She had a lot of fun telling all of us about this. I was very embarrassed and felt humiliated.

The driver of the horses kept telling me, "Jeno, don't pay attention to her. She is stupid." Well I was publicly told that I was an ignorant kid, and she was right. Whether she was stupid or not, she did a great service for me. I took stock in what she said and went searching to improve my life. I can only thank her for the honest words she used, because she put me on a fast track to trying to find an education. I disliked her action and felt resentment toward her for a year or two. I wished she had told me in private, but I am not sure how I would have responded to it.

I rehashed this incident in my mind many times over the years and was eventually able to replace the resentment I felt for her with love, because she'd given me the reason I needed to move on. The truth is what it is, no matter how much it hurts. No pain—no gain. It took several more months to feel comfortable with the love I felt for her. I even danced with her at a holiday dance while I was home from school when I was twenty-one years old. We never talked about the past.

Chapter 21

Almost a Girlfriend

There was another incident that was pushing me to get far away from the village. There was a girl who lived two villages away, who was related to my uncle's wife. I liked the girl, and I used to dance with her at balls. There was a building in her village where farmers used to bring fresh milk. The milk was passed through a centrifugal separator to collect the fat from the milk. The fat portion was purchased by the state from the farmers. She lived in an apartment above this collection facility. Young people from the village used to hang around there every evening, because it was a seven-day operation. I used to go there to talk to her and other people I knew.

One day, she no longer wanted anything to do with me. I could not figure out why, but I accepted it. A few months later, I was told the reason by a young man who had been told by another young man from the village where the girl lived. Some of the young people had staged a show to make it seem as if I was standing under her window making a lot of derogatory statements. I do not know what was said or who said it. I never inquired about it. I did not even know whom I could ask. I could not care less.

I heard that she later vanished while riding her bicycle on the way to the city. She had to go on the bank of a river, and people thought she may have fallen into it. The people were talking about a fifteen-year-old boy who was going on the same road who may have caused her to fall into the river. Her body and her bicycle were never found. I don't know if the police ever investigated it. The river never gave up its secret, if there was any.

This young man's father was coming home late one night, very drunk from the wine cellar. He passed in front of his house, went down into the meadow, and fell and died in three inches of water. "It was God's punishment," some people were saying. The people seemed to connect the two incidents for their own satisfaction. They saw crime and punishment. I think it was just an unfortunate accident. But the gossip went on for months.

I wondered many times what would have happened with me if these young men had not interfered with my life. Both of our lives would have been different. I slowly realized that this was the course of my life. Things had to go wrong for me where I was to make me start to move on. The situation at any place had to become unacceptable for me before I would look for a better one. Some other forces from the spirit world were directing my life.

Chapter 22

Gossip

There was a woman who lived in the same village as the girl who vanished did. She was around forty-one years old. Her husband lived in Budapest, about three hundred miles away, and came back home once or twice a year. He lived his life the way he wanted—far away. When I was around seventeen or eighteen years old, I danced with her at several dances because she was a good dancer.

My father's friend's son moved in with her. When her husband got wind of this, he came home and got into an argument with the young man and stabbed him with a knife. He was taken to the hospital.

A few days later, on a Sunday, I was getting ready to go to a wedding. She showed up at our house. She asked my father if I could go with her to the hospital to visit her housemate, because she was afraid of her husband. My father called me out of the house. He had a big smile on his face and asked me if I wanted to go with her. I said, "No. I am going to the wedding." I really did not want to get in the way of the fighting boyfriend and husband, even though she had an attractive, hot body.

My mother came over to me with big huff and puff two weeks later and said to me, "What am I hearing? The people in the village tell me that you are moving in with that woman."

"Who told you that?" I asked.

"Oh, so and so and so and so," she answered.

"In plain words, it is not true. It is a gossip." Some people must have seen the woman come to our house, and the rumor mill kicked in.

Some young ladies asked me later, "Do you like that woman? What do you like about her?"

"She is a good dancer," I said.

Chapter 23

1950–1952

In the fall of 1950, my brother was twenty-one years old and was drafted into the Hungarian armed forces. I, at the age of seventeen, had to take over all the manual labor on the farm. My father had asthma and could not do much work before having a breathing problem. My mother helped me with some of the work, but her main job was running the household and looking after my six-year-old brother.

My last flare-up of my angry temper occurred in 1951. I was plowing a field with a pair of horses. It was near lunchtime, and the horses were hungry and grabbing after every piece of long grass sticking out of the ground. I could not plow the field correctly because of their jumping around. My temper kicked in. I got angry and kicked one of the horses in the mouth. She started to bleed, and I felt very bad. I verbally apologized to the horses. I let them loose at the end of the field and let them eat grass for about an hour and a half. The injury was not bad. I examined it a day later, and there was no sign of the injury. My father did not like animal abuse. He always said, "They are animals, and they don't have much sense. We have to use our senses to make them do things correctly without abuse and injury."

A new teacher came to our village to teach at the middle school. I used to go over to him and ask him to teach me some mathematics and physics. It was difficult for him to teach me in the evening, because he had to prepare for the next day's class.

Once he asked me to ask all the other fellows in the village who'd missed school because of the war if they wanted to learn; he was going to teach us in the evenings, but no one else wanted to do it.

I heard sometime during the early part of 1952 that there were schools opening in a few major cities specifically for those people who missed receiving an adequate education due to the Second World War. I did not need too much education to be a farmer, but I didn't want to be a farmer. Plus I'd been told I was uneducated. I applied to the state for entrance to the school in May 1952. The state of Hungary sent me information stating that they'd accepted me, but I had to take a qualifying entrance examination. There was also a recommendation required from my grade school teacher, which I received.

I arrived to the specified location in the city of Körmend on the specified day in June and went into the room where the qualifying exam was going to be given. There were six teachers from the Gimnazium at a long table evaluating the candidates. I gave them the papers from the state, and they gave me three pages of paper on which some math and physics problems were written. "Please solve the following problems" was written on the top of the page. I didn't have the slightest idea how to do anything with the problems. The teachers asked me to go up to them when my turn came. I gave them the papers, and they looked at them. The teacher that I assumed was the leader said to me, "We can't send you to the school. You don't know anything."

"That is why I want to go there—because I don't know anything," I said.

The six teachers looked at each other and smiled as if giving a unanimous vote to let me go. The leader of the group said to me,

"You are accepted." He also asked me, "What is your goal in life? What do you want to get an education for?"

I told them, "I want to be a chemist." I did not want to tell them that I wanted to go to school because a girl made fun of my letter writing ability and I felt ignorant and uneducated as compared to younger people.

He also asked me, "What inspired you to want to become a chemist?"

I told him, "The person who collects the milk from the farmers was doing a test to determine the fat content of the milk. I asked him what he was doing. He said it was a chemical process. He inspired me." That was all that came to my mind. I thanked them and left. I was a very happy young man.

The test with the milk did amaze me, but it was not the real reason I was interested in chemistry. The actual reason derived from a conversation I'd had with a cousin who worked in Budapest. I mentioned to him that I want to go to school. He asked me what I wanted to study. I don't remember what I told him. His said to me, "You should study to be a chemist." He told me about what chemists do, and it stuck in my mind.

I received a letter from the state of Hungary in July stating that I was to report to the school in Székesfehérvár on September 12, 1952. Receiving this information was one of the highlights in my life and gave me great happiness. I believe the teachers who evaluated me are now in the spirit world, and I want to thank them for accepting me to the school.

I was facing a difficult problem. My brother was in the army and was not due for discharge until November. Fall was when the harvest had to be finished, the farmland had to be plowed, and the seeds had to be put in the ground for the upcoming year. This is a very labor intensive time on the farm. My father could not physically do the work. My mother could not handle the horses. An able-bodied man was needed to do all the work. But I felt I had to resume my studies if I wanted to make something out of myself. I was supposed to report to the school on September 12. Deep down it hurt me, but I knew I had to leave. There was call, an urge, in me to go and study. We all hoped that as soon I was out of the house, my brother would be let go from the army. It would take about three weeks to notify the army and process the discharge papers.

I also knew my uncles would help my parents until my brother was back. With that in mind, I packed my bags on September 10. My father asked me on September 11 if I was leaving, and I said yes. He gave me one dollars' worth of Hungarian currency and wished me good luck. I also had twenty dollars' worth of Hungarian currency that I'd saved during the previous year. Carrying my suitcase, I walked to the train station, which was about five kilometers away from my home. I did not know anything about the train schedules. I bought a ticket to the city where I had to go and boarded a train to go to the next city where I supposed change train. There was no train that evening to the city where I needed to go.

There was a rectory about five minutes walking distance from the railroad station I arrived at. The priest who was in charge of the rectory had been a parish priest in our area. We used to provide transportation for him with our coach and horses. Since I could go no further by train that evening, I went over to the rectory and asked if they could provide shelter for me for the night. I told him where I was going and why. First he told me that there was a place at the railroad station for people who had to stay overnight. I was totally ignorant of that too. So I mentioned to him that I had not known that. He said, "Wait here a minute," and walked out.

He came back in about five minutes with a nun. They brought some blankets and told me I could stay and sleep in the office. He asked me when my train was leaving, and I told him the time. He said they would wake me up in ample time to catch the train.

They did wake me up in time, and a short time later I was at the railroad station again.

The train pulled in about half hour later, and the conductor announced the cities where the train would stop and its final destination. The travelers got on the train. The conductors blew the whistles and waved their arms to the engineer, and the train started to move.

A female conductor, who looked like she was my age, came to me about ten minutes later and asked me for my ticket. She looked at it and then she looked at me again and said, "This ticket is no good."

"Why not?" I asked her.

"This was for yesterday," she said.

"Yes. There was no train going yesterday evening," I said.

"Yesterday evening you were supposed to go to the ticket counter and ask for a replacement ticket for today," she said.

"I am sorry, but I did not know," I said. She asked me where I was from and why I was going to the city. I told her that I was going to school.

"I am going to keep the ticket and let you know when to get off. If anybody asks you for the ticket, tell them I have it," she said. She started to walk away and then turned around and said, "Good luck to you."

I thanked her for the well wishes. I think she thought I was a nineteen-year-old, ignorant young man from a farm who had never traveled on a train before. She came to me as the train was pulling into my destination. The wheels screeched as the train slowly came to a stop.

"This is where you get off. Here is your ticket."

I said, "Thank you." I walked off the train with my suitcase in my hand.

There were three other young men looking around. Each of us had some suitcases, and nobody seemed to be expecting us. One of the fellows asked me, "Where are you going?"

I told him the address of the school and the reason I was going there.

The other two overheard me, and one of them said, "We are going there too."

The person who asked me the question said, "I am going there too."

The four of us got into a horse and buggy taxi, and the driver took us to the school.

We paid the driver and went into the school.

This was the start of my new and different life.

Chapter 24

I Get Educated

We arrived at the dormitory where we were to live for the next two years. It was a large square building. It had four floors, a large dining area, and a large study hall with exits to two streets. It had about 150 rooms for sleeping purposes, which could hold about one thousand students. The building used to be a seminary, so religious paintings had adorned the walls of every room. One of the teachers told us that all the walls in every room were painted over with white oil paint after the state took it over. He said that he felt bad about the repainting of the rooms.

The school we attended for eleven months of the year was a Gimnazium. We had to take a test to determine our position, and our progress was monitored during the year. My schedule was heavily loaded with chemistry, physics, and mathematics. The classes for those of us who were returning to our school careers were held in the afternoons, from 1:00 to 5:00 p.m. The morning classes, which ran from 8:00 a.m. to 12:00 noon, were for the younger regular students. We had the same teachers teaching the same subjects to us as to the morning classes, except we were being taught at an accelerated rate. We had lots of homework to do. We had to complete the four years' workload in two years. Only the highest performing students were going to be able to go to the university for higher education.

Our teachers were very good. They took extra effort to teach us the necessary tricks to learn fast and to retain what we learned. I am grateful for the extra effort and time they put into teaching us. They took pride in our success. I wish them success, wherever they are. My math teacher was very proud of me because of my reasoning problem-solving ability.

Ten other students and I attended airborne training and glider flying training for recreational purposes on weekends. I was able to jump from an airplane only once, because an appendix operation halted any further attempts. I had an attack of abdominal pain and vomiting one Saturday night in the fall of 1953. The students alerted the dormitory attendant, who called an ambulance to take me to the hospital. I was diagnosed with acute appendicitis. I was operated on the following Monday morning. The doctor who did the operation told me that the appendix did not seem to have any problem.

I was in a room with five other people. One of my biggest problems was I could not urinate when people were around me. The day after the operation, I had to urinate and so the nurse handed me a urinal. I started to have pain from the urine accumulating in my bladder. I told her that I could not use it, and I had to go to the bathroom. I proceeded to get out of the bed and was going to walk to the bathroom. She probably went to get the doctor, because as I was nearing the door, the doctor was running toward me. He was yelling, "What are you trying to do to me?"

"I don't want to do anything to you," I said. "I desperately need to urinate, and I cannot do it in the room. I am in pain, and I have to go to the bathroom."

"Okay, I'll follow you," he said. The bathroom was outside the room just down the hallway. He came with me and stayed outside. He followed me back to my bed and then left. The next day, he brought five other doctors to my bed and told them that I'd walked to the bathroom the day after the operation.

The hospital food was creamy mashed potatoes or thick, creamy soup. Everything they served was creamy, and I could not stand creamy food. I asked my classmate to bring in some food from the dormitory: chicken, baked potatoes, and pastries. I was not supposed to eat that kind of food, but I did—and it was great. I was in the hospital for five days after the operation. The hospital discharged me on the sixth day, and I walked five kilometers back to my dormitory.

I was no longer going to be jumping out of airplanes, and I had not received a permit to fly gliders alone.

There was another incident where my temper got in my way. A classmate of mine and I were at a movie theater. We were waiting for a show to end, and we were going into the next show. I always had a smile on my face, like a dolphin. There was a good-looking young girl behind concession counter. I was looking at her, and she said to me, "Don't just smile at me. Bring back the bottle that you took. You were supposed to bring it back."

"I didn't take any bottle from you," I said to her.

"Yes, you did," she insisted.

I got a kind of angry and said to her, "If you think I took it, why don't you call the police?"

My classmate said to me, "Jeno, don't get upset. She was probably only trying to get friendly with you." I felt bad about my anger. She did not say anything. The people came out of the show, and we went in to see the next performance.

I saw the girl a week later at a restaurant. I tried to apologize, but she would not listen. My sudden anger probably had to do with an incident that took place when I was about fifteen years old.

There were religious cards describing various points of Jesus going to the crucifixion. These cards used to be exchanged between the women in the village. My mother asked me to take her card to a woman who lived in the middle of the village. I took the card to her house. She was not home, but the door to her house was open. I waited around for her. While I was waiting, another fellow showed up. He was two years younger than I was, and he was a smoker. He had a cigarette but no match. This woman had a fire going in her stove, which you could see from outside. The fellow asked me if I would light up his cigarette with the fire in the stove. About five minutes later, the woman showed up from across the street. I gave her the card and left.

The woman came to our house the next day and told my father that I'd stolen ten forint from her. My father took me aside, gave me a couple slaps on the face, and questioned me—a standard interrogation. I told her what happened at the house and that I had not taken any of her money. My father told her that he did not believe I took the money.

"I will take a better look at the place," she said. She came back the next day and told us that she'd found the money. She was very apologetic. "The money fell behind something," she said.

She needs something, I thought to myself. At least she came and told us that the money had been found.

My class graduated after two years of training, earning our high school diplomas in July 1954. I received the highest level of achievement among the approximately 950 graduating students. At the graduation ceremony, I was called upon to tell approximately 1000 people how I'd reached the top level. I could hardly speak. I was not prepared. No one had told me that I would have to make a statement.

I was accepted to the University of Natural Sciences in Budapest to study to be a research chemist. I reported to the university in September 1954.

The first year went without any major incident. I did learn a fact that I'd wished I'd known eight years earlier. The inorganic chemistry professor was teaching about the properties of all the elements. When he got to gold, he told us that in the United States, gold was sold in commerce in one-ounce packages in powder form. The gold was wrapped in white paper, which was wrapped in blue paper in about four-by-two inch packages. When I heard this, my jaw fell open and I had a flashback.

My grandfather, on my mother's side, lived in the United States for a few years during the late 1920s or the early 1930s. He used to work for a stone crushing company. I do not know any other details about it. He brought a footlocker with him when he came home. My grandmother gave this footlocker to my mother. It was put up with a bunch of other things in the attic of our new house. I was about fourteen years old at the time, and I used to look through all these things in the attic to see if I could find anything interesting. One day I opened the footlocker, and I found a box that was about twelve-inches long by six-inches wide and six-inches tall. The box was full of blue paper packages. I opened one of the blue packages; inside was a white paper package, and inside that was yellow powder. I thought it was used for gold paint. The packages were quite heavy compared to the size. I told my father that I found this yellow gold powder, and I asked if it would be alright if I put it in linseed oil and painted the picture frames and the metal parts of the petroleum lamps we had with it.

He said, "Yes, sure."

I put all the powder into two gallons of linseed oil and painted away. I noticed that I had to mix it constantly, because the powder would sink to the bottom. It did not behave the same way as the regular gold paint I'd seen other people use. I painted as much as I could and then closed the cans and put them away. Most of the powder stayed in the linseed oil at the bottom of the can forever.

When I was about eight years old, I got hold of a two-inch-high ceramic figure of a little boy holding a gold ring. I broke the figure to get the gold ring out. I discovered there was no gold ring, only pieces of painted ceramic. I was very disappointed. About six years later, I'd held a few pounds of gold in my hand and did not recognize it. I did not know what gold looked like in powdered form.

My first year studies concluded at the university in June 1955. All the male students had to report to military service. We were in the Reserve Officers' Training Corps. We spent the month of July at a boot camp.

I went home at the end of July 1955 and looked for the items that I'd painted with the real gold in 1947. They were all gone. The linseed oil had dried up in the cans, and my brother discarded them. He did not remember where he'd thrown them. The picture frames had been replaced by new ones. The petroleum lamps had been replaced by electric lights. It looked like it was a cosmic conspiracy designed so we'd never recover the gold.

Maybe it was a good thing, because it was illegal to own any gold in Hungary at that time. One could be prosecuted for ownership and the gold would be confiscated. We'd heard of people who were accused of hoarding gold and were prosecuted and abused by the police. Two of my parents' Jewish friends died in prison because they were accused of hoarding gold.

I was still looking for something that needed to be corrected.

Chapter 25

Chicago: The Wonderful Town

In the middle of June 1958, the spirit voices told me to go to Chicago and I would find a job there. I still had about $50.00, so I bought a one-way bus ticket for $6.50 for the Trail-Ways Lines to Chicago. The ride took about thirty-six hours. I was kind of confused when I arrived to Chicago. I stayed in a nearby hotel for four days and kept looking for the job I was hoping to get.

Around the end of June, I called a Hungarian radio station to inquire if they'd had anyone advertising for help. The lady to whom I spoke said she didn't know of any open positions but wished me good luck. I needed some good luck alright—and plenty of it. I was almost out of money. I stayed around the bus terminal for three or four days and slept on the chairs and benches, but eventually I had to move on. The employees of the terminal said I could not stay around there. Some people suggested I go to the Salvation Army, telling me they probably could help me. Interestingly, the Salvation Army refused to help me; they did not even offer me food. They probably thought I was a freeloader. Meanwhile, in my mind the voices told me to go to Canada. This was getting a little bit too much to deal with. I think some of these voices were being sarcastic. I went into a police station and told three policemen that the voices in my head were telling me to go to Canada. Two of the policemen left and the third told me that they could not help me, but he gave me three aspirins. I guess it was not the policemen's job to help anyone in this type of situation. The situation probably appeared differently to them than to me.

I met someone who told me to go to a specific bar, whose owner was Hungarian, and they would give me work. I do not remember where and how I met this person or the name of the bar. It was a fairly large building in the middle of a city block. I went inside. On the right side was a curved bar with several people sitting at it. On the left side were two other rooms that served as restaurant seating for up to seventy-five people. I asked the bartender for the owner, and he pointed out a man and said, "Mike is in charge." I told the man I needed a job and that I did not have any money or any place to stay. He asked me where I came from and why I had come to Chicago. I told him that I could not find a job in New York and was trying to make it in Chicago instead. We talked for a while about where we each came from. He told me that the bar belonged to his uncle, who was getting up there in age and was not that healthy; therefore, Mike was running the restaurant and the bar.

After an hour of information exchange, he gave me a job as a waiter. There were three other young men like me working as waiters. He gave me some blankets and pillows and an old mattress on the floor to sleep on in a room behind the bar. All four of us slept in the same room. The other three men told me that they had been working there for about a month and a half, but they had not been paid yet and Mike did not treat them well at all. They said it was almost like being a slave.

I was happy to have a job, to have food to eat, and to not have to sleep on the street. I worked there for a few weeks. But ultimately, there was no rest in my mind. I started to feel uncomfortable with the situation, and I thought I should move on. The spirit voices did not bother me at first, but after a few days they pointed out that I still had to find something that needed to be corrected. I still had no idea what that could be. The communication was not very good, because my mind seemed to be focused on everyday events.

I did not like what was happening at the bar and how the other workers were treated. After four weeks, I decided to go back to New York City. I asked Mike to give me my pay. He said okay. A few days later, he still had not given it to me. I asked him again. He asked me, "Why are you in such a rush to leave?"

"I am going back to New York City," I answered him. He gave me my pay after I asked him the third time. I took the bus to New York City the next day. I thought I would find what I needed there.

Chapter 26

I Was a Runaway

I think the spirits knew that if they instigated me to cross the border to Canada, my mind would bring back this episode. Today, as I am writing, I am 100 percent convinced that is the reason they did it.

The spirits were correct; I got a job in Chicago. But I think their concern was for me to think about the incident when I ran away from home. They probably wanted to know how I felt about the police force. They were going to correct anything if there was a need for correction. I was in good hands. I just did not know it.

Our house on the farm in Hungary was on a four acres lot about three hundred yards from the neighbors and positioned next to a large pine forest. I was about sixteen years old. It was November, and the air was not too cold yet. We could work outside without gloves or overcoats. My brother and I were supposed to go out to the forest and bring some firewood home. He and I got into an argument over who would go get the tools we needed to take with us. He got angry and threw a five-feet-long chain at me. The chain hit my arm. I, being quick tempered, picked up a stick that was about three feet long and approximately two inches in diameter. He was walking away from me, and I threw the stick at him. The stick hit him in the back of the leg, and he collapsed. I thought

I broke his leg. I was so afraid of my father's anger, I ran away. I left without money, overcoat, gloves, or a hat. All I had was the thick curly hair on my head.

This was probably a stupid thing to do, but in the long run, it had a very important place in my life. I was a stubborn person. I do not know what got into me—probably nature's correction facilities were at work. I ran out through the backyard door, down to the forest, and got on the highway about one hundred yards away. I wanted to get out of Hungary. I walked about six kilometers to the nearest railroad station in Nádasd. I got on the train going south toward Yugoslavia. I'd heard that people who wanted to get out of Hungary went to Öriszentpéter. The village was near the border of Yugoslavia. This area was not guarded as heavily as the Austrian border, because Yugoslavia was a communist country. This train was going that way.

Shortly after the train started to go, the conductor came and asked for my ticket. I did not have one, so he put me off at the next stop. I had relatives within three kilometers from this station, but I was not interested in going there. There was a Gypsy community in the area, and I just happened to go to a house where a single old Gypsy lived. He had a good fire going in the stove, and he let me stay there for a while. I was able to keep warm while I waited for the next train to arrive in about four hours so I could continue my trip. The passenger trains on this line were always short four to six cars. I boarded the next train, and within five minutes the conductor came and asked me for my ticket. I did not have one, so he put me off the train at the next stop in Pankasz.

I had not eaten at all that day, and I was very hungry. I'd never begged in my life, but the hunger was so strong in me that my pride just evaporated. I went up to a house. There was a man and his wife in the home; they appeared to be in their early forties. I asked them if they would give me some food. The woman looked at her husband, and he told her give me some soup and bread. She gave me a large bowl of tomato-turnip soup and a large slice of bread. I'd never liked this type of soup, but boy did it taste good that day. They must have just finished eating, because the soup was still warm. They did not ask me anything. They probably thought the less they knew, the better off they were. I finished the soup and asked the man if he would let me sleep in the stable with the animals. He took me out and showed me where I could sleep in the hay in the stable. There were about eight cows and about ten sheep in there. The sheep were fenced into a separate area. I went to sleep in the straw with my clothes on. I woke up at my usual time, about seven o'clock in the morning, and left. I don't know if they saw me leaving or not.

Őriszentpéter was just five kilometers away. I was getting close to the village, and I saw two policemen on bicycles further down the road. I saw about five houses on the left side of the road and went over to one of them. The occupants were Gypsies too. As I got to the house, two men from other houses came to the house I went into. I asked them if they could help me get out of the country. These guys started to talk in their Gypsy language. I suddenly saw in my mind a human body with the head cut off; the body was bleeding at the neck, and blood was all over the ground. This vision scared the living daylights out of me. The men had not touched me yet. I had the utmost urge to get out of there. I asked them where the toilet was; I knew it was outside, and I hoped I could get away before they could grab me. My senses were telling me that these men were dangerous. One of them pointed toward the outhouse, which was about fifty yards from the house. I got out of the house and ran over the railroad tracks to the highway. At that point, I felt relatively safe.

I went into the village to the railroad station. The station was large, because lots of lumber was produced in this area. I went inside and was looking around, contemplating what to do next. As I was walking around inside the station, I saw three of the Gypsies I'd run from. They kept following me around—not very closely, but keeping me in eyesight.

There were two side streets to the main drag. I left the station and went down one side street and came back on the other. Wherever I went, the three gypsies were only a short distance away. I was very concerned that these idiot Gypsies thought that I had money and would kill me to try to get it. I was actually afraid of them. Suddenly, I realized that I did not know anybody around there. I did not have any help. I needed food, clothing, and some sensible direction to get out of the country. The temperature was dropping, and I felt hungry and cold.

I got tired of the situation around noon, and I went into the shop of a tailor and asked him if I could stay and warm up. He said yes. He had a wood-burning stove, and I sat next to it. The warmth felt really good to my body. He did not ask me anything, and soon I learned why. He was working mainly for the police officers. They were coming in and out of his shop all the time. I saw the Gypsies in front of the store a couple of times. The tailor knew that something was not right with me. After about two hours, he asked me to leave. He said, "Too many policemen are around here and asked me who you are. Maybe you should go home."

I left, but the Gypsies were following me again. Earlier in the day, I'd noticed that there was a police officer's residency down the road. I was scared for my life, so I decided to go into the police station to get away from the Gypsies. I went into the police residency and told them that the Gypsies were following me and I was afraid of them and I want to go home. They went out and looked, but they did not see them. The place was very nice. The house appeared to have three floors. The hallway walls were tiled. The house originally belonged to the owner of the sawmill that was nearby; it was confiscated by the government because he was wealthy. The police officers lived in it now. There was a lieutenant, three sergeants with different ranks, two corporals, and a few privates. The lieutenant and the sergeants started to interrogate me. The lieutenant told me to take everything out of my pockets. I emptied the contents of my pockets onto the table: one handkerchief, one small pocket knife, one expended rifle shell with the bullet in it, and a half of a lead water faucet handle that was shaped slightly like a brass knuckle. My father advised me not to carry that lead faucet around and said I should not use it if I got into a fight. First of all, somebody could grab my hand and break my fingers with it if the person wanted to take it away. Secondly, the lead was soft, so if I hit someone with it on it would collapse onto my fingers and could break them. He suggested to me that I throw it away. Now I was wishing I had done that.

The interrogation started out with questions. "How did you get here?" asked the lieutenant.

"I took the train to Riman, and the conductor put me off here," I answered.

"What does the railroad station sign say at Riman?" he asked.

"Riman," I said.

"What does the railroad station sign say at Riman?" he asked again.

"Riman," I repeated.

He asked me twice more.

I gave the same answer twice.

"No," he said. "You were never there! The sign says Szöce-Zalaháságy."

Interestingly, I'd been at that railroad station several times before because we had relatives at Szöce, but I'd never looked at the railroad station sign. Everybody called it Riman. The village was called Riman, but the railroad station sign was different.

I described again to them how I'd arrived there. I was probably guilty of whatever they had in their mind. I told them why I'd ran away and that I never read the sign. Of course, they did not believe me. There were inconsistencies in my statement. There were two mistakes made. First, I should have told them I never looked at the sign. Second, he should have asked me if I looked at the sign.

"Did you kill someone?" one of the policemen asked.

"No," I replied. "Why would I come in here if I killed somebody?"

One of the sergeants said, "You have that faucet piece in your pocket because you want to get out of the country, and if you meet a border patrol you can use it to knock him out." This was an interesting thought; however, it had never entered my mind. The last person I wanted to see was a border patrol.

"Did you burn down somebody's house?"

"No way," I said.

They were determined to get to the truth. I did not know what they thought the truth was, but they were looking for it. The lieutenant picked up a three-feet-long metal piece used for cleaning rifle barrels. He told me to bend down. Wow I thought to myself. I better be prepared for a good beating.

The lieutenant kept hitting my romp and demanding the truth. Just then a higher ranking sergeant—who'd just gotten off duty—came in and asked, "Who is he?" They told him that I just came in by myself and I was a runaway.

"What is your name?" he asked.

"Jeno Papp," I said.

"Where are you from?"

"Nagymizdo," I answered.

"Do you know Lajcsi Papp?" he asked eagerly.

"Yes, he is my cousin," I answered.

"I am his wife's cousin," he said. "Were you at the wedding?"

"Yes," I said, "but I do not remember seeing you there."

"I could not make it to the wedding, because I was on duty and we were short staffed here," he said. At that moment, they were all satisfied with my identity. They turned me over to him to take care of me. I do not know his real name, so I will call him Karoly.

"Go out to the hallway and wait," he said. He came out about ten minutes later. "Come with me." We went into a side room, and he said, "Turn around and pull your pants and underwear down. I want to see what they did to you." I did what he asked. He looked at my behind and said,

"We can't let you go until the bruises are gone, probably a week or two. Is that okay?"

"Yes," I agreed.

He took me out to the hallway again and showed me a bed. "You can sleep here at night," he said. I had to sleep on my stomach the next two nights because of the pain in my backside. During the day, I had to sit on a padded chair. These law enforcers had become law abusers.

Karoly took me into the kitchen and introduced me to the cook and said, "Help her with whatever you can." I chopped wood, brought in water from an outside well, and took the garbage out for the next seven days. The officers were pretty good to me afterward.

A week later, Karoly looked at my butt again and said it looked better. He and another police officer took me over to the police station, where the head of the police department was with all the administrative staff and their offices. There was a one-room jail, which was housing a prisoner. He'd just finished chopping wood for the stoves when we arrived there. The weather was getting colder, and the clouds were gathering. Karoly said to me, "Go inside the jail with that fellow. It is warm in there. I will get you when we finish the paperwork."

The jail had a stove and two beds, made from wood, in the room and a fairly large window with thick metal bars across it. There was no way to open the door from inside. It was kind of scary to me. About fifteen minutes later, Karoly came and said, "Come, Jeno. The paperwork is done, and the captain wants to see you."

Karoly opened the door to the captain's office, and he told us to come in. The captain was a huge man. His upper body was about two times wider than mine, and one of his fists was about three times bigger than one of my fist. I don't think I'd ever seen a man that large. He said, "Here is a transfer letter. You give it to the police department in Körmend. They are expecting you." He then gave me a lecture about good behavior. He had a deep voice, and the longer he spoke, the louder he got. I do not remember most of what he said, except for the last warning: "If you ever come back here and cause trouble, I will tear you into pieces. I can do that. You can see it from my size. Do you understand?"

"Yes, sir, I do," I said.

His voice, his body, his words, and the place left an everlasting impression in me. I think they wanted to scare me to make sure I went home. I took the paper from him, and the three of us went back to the police officers' residency. We had dinner. Karoly said to me, "Let's go to the railroad station," which was about a five to ten minute walk from the police officers' residency. For some reason only they knew, they wanted to get rid of me that evening. There was no passenger train leaving until next morning, but a freight train carrying lumber was about to leave the station.

"Get on this one here," Karoly said. There was a car that had some empty area on the outside.

"The train inspector will put me off," I said.

"No, he won't. I will talk to him," Karoly said.

"Good," I said. I got on the train, and he left. Within ten minutes, the inspector showed up with a lamp in his hand.

"Where are you going?" he asked me.

"I want to go to Körmend," I said.

"Get off the train," he demanded.

I jumped off and walked away. I wondered if Karoly really talked to him. He probably did not care where I was going as long as I was off his hands. The inspector must have seen me getting on, because as soon as I got off he started to wave his light and the train started to leave. I could not get back on it. It probably happened for the best. It would have been very cold on the train. I did not even know where it was going.

I was stuck alone in the dark and near the Gypsies. I ran for two reasons: one, to keep warm, and two, to get far away from that place. I made it all the way to the village of Pankasz, where I'd slept before.

There was a bar near the edge of the village. The light was on, and I went in. The time was about nine o'clock at night. There were two young men playing cards. I sat down next to them and watched them play. About an hour later, one of them was winning and bought me glass of wine. *It's great,* I thought to myself. I was wishing for another glass of wine, but he did not offer me anymore. Twelve o'clock midnight came. The bar closed. The two card players went home. I went back to the house where I'd slept before. I snuck into the stable and slept there in the hay with cows and sheep until daybreak. I was out of the stable by 5:00 a.m., as the clock on the nearby church indicated. I did not want anybody to know that I'd slept there. It probably was a good thing that the inspector took me off the train; this way, I was able to get a few hours of sleep.

I went over to the railroad station and inquired about the fare to Körmend. The ticket schedule showed the fare was four forint and fifty fillér. The train was leaving at 8:00 a.m., and I had no money. I knew I would be put off the train without a ticket. I had to come up with the money somehow. There was a church nearby, and next to the church was the rectory where the priest lived. I thought the priest might give me money for the fare. It started to snow slowly. I went over to the rectory and knocked on the door. The housekeeper answered the door. I explained to the woman what had happened to me and that I need money for the train to go home. She asked the priest to come over. I told him my misery.

"It is winter. Don't you have an overcoat?" he asked.

"No," I replied.

"How much is the train fare?" he asked me.

"It cost four forint and fifty fillér," I said.

He thought for a second and then gave me five forint. I ran to the station, bought a ticket, and got on the train. When the train started to move around eight o'clock that morning, I felt happier.

It was snowing fairly heavily when the train pulled into the railroad station in Körmend at around ten thirty that morning. I got off the train and went over to the police station. I went into the office and gave the transfer letter that the police had given me in Öriszentpéter to the secretary, who was also a police officer. He gave it to the captain, who was standing nearby. He looked at it and went into his office. One of the officers took me to another room, where several police officers were eating lunch. Two of these policemen knew me.

"What are you doing here?" they asked me. I told them about my excursion. "Did you eat anything today?" they asked.

"No," I replied. They gave me some food and told me to wait in that room until they finished what they had to do. Everything had to be documented, and the case had to be closed. An officer called me into the captain's office around four in the afternoon.

"Read this paper, sign it, and you can go home," the secretary said to me. The paper he was referring to said that I did not do anything wrong and that I was not abused by the members of the police department. I signed the paper and was allowed to go home.

I was happy that I did not get the same treatment my older brother had once received. He was beaten so badly by two drunken policemen that he had two inches of swelling on his head. He could not see for two weeks. The swelling was traveled down his body for about a month before it finally was gone. The two policemen and the police department were sued, and they had to pay a considerable amount of money to him. The two policemen were from this location. That is why I had to sign the paper. I could not prove that they had beaten me up and I'd recovered without any problem.

About four inches of snow fell during the day. The snow was

tapering off, and it was getting much colder. I started to make the six kilometers journey home on the road by the Rába River and across the meadow. I followed the tracks of the people who had earlier gone to the market. Halfway home, I noticed that my shoes were frozen and were not bending anymore. My feet were warm inside, and I made quicker steps to keep warm. It took me about two and a half hours to get home.

Our dog was waiting for me at the front gate. My biggest surprise was that he seemed to know I was coming home. He could not hear my footsteps, as there was snow on the ground. He was greeting me with his tail wagging, friendly yapping barks, and jumping on me as I walked through the front gate. He seemed to be saying, "Welcome home, boy." I went into the stable and wanted to go to sleep in the hay. My father came out of the house into the stable within five minutes. He was calling my name as he opened the door.

"Jeno, is that you?" he asked.

"Yes," I answered him.

"I knew from the dog's barking that you had come home," my father said. "Come in the house." I went inside. My mother was putting food out for me as I went in. "Where were you?" my father asked me.

"Öriszentpéter," I said.

"We thought you were at the relatives in Szöce," he said.

"No," I replied.

I never told anyone what had happened to me during those twelve days. Nobody ever asked me about it. I was not a bragger, and it was not in my blood to give away information. It was my private lesson in life.

My father seemed to have extraordinary senses. He sensed things ahead of time. He was aware of things when they were out of tune. He seemed to have premonitions about things—more than I can ever imagine.

Chapter 27

Back in New York

When I arrived back in New York City, I went to the Hungarian restaurant on Broad Street, where I used to eat many times when I was at Columbia University. I ran into an acquaintance of mine from Washington DC at the restaurant. He asked me if I had a job. I told him that I did not have one. He said to me, "A lot of things depend on you."

"I know," I said.

He suggested I go to my sponsor, who'd helped me when I came to the United States. Interestingly, I'd never thought to do that. I wanted to be independent and able to look after my needs. Unfortunately, I was not able to do that in the big city of New York.

The next day, I went over to the World Wide Catholic Charity (WWCC) on Fifth Avenue in New York City. I think they had a record of me, because they gave me two dollars a day, sent me for job interviews, and gave me a room in a hotel on 31st Street.

I was at an interview for a job that had to do with chemistry, but the interviewer did not think I was sufficiently versatile in English for the job. He sent me to another manager, who was in charge of manual laborers. He asked me about my education and said, "We do not have any job here. The man who sent you here is stupid. I am really sorry, but he should have hired you. He probably did not like you personally."

I used to hang around bars on 34th Street. One time, one of the ladies of the night asked me to come and live with her and be her pimp. She said, "Whatever you want, I will do it for you." This was quit an offer considering the money and sex. I had thought about it for about an hour. I would have free access to all the STDs—what a deal. Therefore, I turned her down. I thought, *If I ever get married, I want to have healthy children.* I did not have any desire for sexually transmittable diseases. Sometimes I wonder how my life would have turned out if I'd taken her up on her offer.

I was a very heavy smoker, sometimes smoking more than two packs a day. I was very, very tired because of the limited sleep and food I had consumed in the last seven months, the constant walking to job interviews, too much smoking, and the mental anguish I was going through. The situation was going from bad to worse. Each day, I had to wait at the WWCC for about three to four hours before they would give me the two dollars. I was falling asleep everywhere due to the fact that I was exhausted. One day, a man from the WWCC came out into the waiting area and said to me, "We are not giving you any more money."

I asked, "Why?"

"You are working during the night. That is why you are sleeping here when you come to collect money from us," was his answer. I told him I was not working, but he did not want to hear it. It was just one more day when I did not eat ... and more were to come.

I met a Hungarian electrical engineer. I do not remember his name. I believe he came from Germany or France. He was offered a job in the States because of his extensive knowledge connecting different power generating systems into a power grid. We were staying in the same hotel. He only stayed in New York City for about three weeks before moving on for his job. He received some money from the company he was going to work for, and he used to buy me food once a day in the Horn & Hardart, an automat restaurant, while he was around. One day, he no longer answered the knock on his door; I heard that he'd left that morning. I used to stare at the food-serving places and wish that someone would give me something to eat. Most of the people did not know how hungry I was, and some of them probably did not care. Once I asked a waiter to give me some soup. He said, "Go get a job." *I wish I could*, I thought. Sometimes the people who served hot dogs and hamburgers at the corner of 42nd Street and Broadway would give me a hotdog or two.

There was a fellow I knew who was going back to Hungary, because he could not handle the situation in the States. Whatever problem he had, he did not tell me about it, and I did not ask him about it. I did not really want to know. He was spending a few weeks in New York City before departing. We used to spend some time together, and he would pay for food so we could eat together. He told me about the kind of life he'd had in Hungary. I could not figure out why he was going back. He was under the supervision of the WWCC until he left the United States. He had money, but I do not know whether he received any money from the WWCC. I mentioned to him that it takes a few weeks for a man to starve to death, even in a big city like New York.

One day I was sleeping still at about ten in the morning, when someone started pounding on my door and calling my name. I opened the door, and there was my friend with coffee and some cheese pastry. He said he was worried about me and was going over to the WWCC to give them some advise. I got a telephone call within the hour from the WWCC telling me to come over, because they wanted to talk to me.

Chapter 28

Bellevue Hospital

The people at the WWCC asked me to go over to the hospital to see if there was anything wrong with me, because I was sleeping too much. I saw a doctor at Bellevue Hospital. He may have been a psychiatrist. He asked me if I wanted to stay in the hospital. I said yes. I had not eaten much for several days, and I thought at least I would get some food. I wanted to rest, eat, and not to worry about anything for a while. They put me into a place, which had three rooms connected by two doorways. One large room had two Ping-Pong tables in it, and several people were playing the game. The middle large room had around twenty-five card tables in it. Several people were playing different card games. The first large room had one longer table and several smaller tables. This room also served as a dining room and a staging/observation area. They assigned beds to us in smaller rooms—a different beds each night. I saw mice running around the rooms during the night. I understood and spoke some English but not enough to keep me out of trouble. I slept about 80 percent of the time for about a week.

There were full-time nurses on duty at all times and student nurses on training part of the day, usually in the afternoon. The staff nurses seemed to always be busy with their jobs, but the student nurses were freer. I started to like one of the student nurses a lot. She was nice and very good looking. Her grandparents were from Hungary and lived in upstate New York. I wanted to get involved with her. She gave me her school address and asked me to write to her later.

I got involved in playing table tennis and several different card games and board games. The student nurses joined in the games when they were free. I overheard someone ask one of the nurses how and what I was doing. She answered him, "He is sleeping most of the time."

There were two chemists in the hospital with me. One was missing an arm. We talked sometimes about chemistry and other sciences. These chemists told me that the people in the unit were under observation for psychological problem, but they were there for some other reason, which they did not specify. I did not ask or care to know the reasons why anybody was there. Living on the streets of New York City for months wears a person out.

I was interviewed by a woman. I presume she was a psychiatrist. She asked me if something was bothering me, if I had any concerns, and why I was there. I do not remember the details of the conversation. She wrote things down as we were talking. Looking back, I probably did not understand 50 percent of what she said. At the time I thought I did, but over the years I learned that a word or a statement may mean different things to the person who speaks it and the person who hears it. I'd heard many times, "I hear you, but I don't know what you mean."

There were a couple of things that stuck in my mind about this interview. She was very nervous. Her hand was shaking as she was writing. I wondered what was wrong with her. As it turned out, she was determining and evaluating what was wrong with me. I had a concern I shared with her. I'd met a Hungarian fellow who was around the same age as me about three months before. He told me that we had to report to the selective service system for military service. He was in the military, and he said, he had to take a lie detector test when he reported. He did not know what the name of the instrument was called, so he called it a "lying machine." He described what the operator of the instrument did and what questions were asked of him. I tried to explain to her that I was apprehensive about the test. Could this instrument give wrong information? I don't know why I was so apprehensive. I did not belong to any political party in Hungary that would have been classified as subversive in the United States. With my very poor, broken English explanation, though, I got myself into one of the worst situation a person can get in. I thought I knew enough English that I could get by in the United States, but I did not. I sure could not explain myself correctly and was easily misunderstood. I did not know that my English skills—or rather my lack of them—was causing a problem. I found this out two months later.

Interestingly, the spirit communicators left me alone for over a month.

Chapter 29

Pilgrim State Hospital

About two weeks after the interview, they transferred me to the Pilgrim State Hospital in Long Island. I had to pick up my two suitcases from the hotel room where I'd stayed on 31st Street.

They transferred me because of whatever the psychiatrist wrote in her report. They took me to a star-shaped building with four floors on each wing. One wing was for women, the second was for old people who couldn't care for themselves, and the third was for people who were under observation to determine what was wrong with them. It was a sorting place to observe behavior and determine medical treatment needed. Some patients were let go after treatment; some were transferred to other buildings for long-term stays.

A few days after I arrived, I met a Hungarian doctor there. I suppose he was a psychiatrist.

He asked me. "Do you know where you are?"

"No," I said.

He said to me, "This is a mental institution, you know." He asked me, "Do you know why you are here?"

"No, I do not," I said.

"We will see if anything is wrong," he told me. I do not remember what my response was, but I really did not care where

I was. It was better there than sitting hungry somewhere in New York City. At least I had a place to sleep and food to eat.

I talked to three different psychiatrists. They all asked me why I was there. "I do not know," was my answer to each of them. I really did not know, fortunately or unfortunately. They asked me what religion I belonged to. I told them I was catholic; therefore, I had to talk to a catholic priest. They all were very nice and told me they wanted to help me. I just did not know what kind of help I needed. I was too worn out and too tired to care.

My senses were telling me that I was facing a big problem, and I had to be very careful of what I said. I tried to be careful and not talk about things that people wouldn't be able to understand. There can be no discussion or communication if people do not understand each other.

There was a guiding situation from my past in Hungary that came to my mind. I was at a medical center. There was a man ahead of me who was there for an examination. He did not appear to be an educated man. He went in to see the doctor for whatever ailment he had. When he came out about twenty minutes later, he was very agitated and angry. He was coming toward me and was muttering a few cursing words and said to me, "I am going back and punching him in the nose!" He turned and went back toward the door that he'd just came out off.

"Hold on, hold on! Wait a minute, man," I said as I was rushing to him. I urged him to stop. "What did he do? What did he say? Why do you want to punch him in the nose?" I asked him.

"He cursed me," he said.

I could not believe that. "Just what did he say exactly?" I asked him.

"Your sacrament," he said. This is a cursing statement in most areas in Hungary, but pronounced slightly differently. That is what he'd heard—but it is not necessarily true that it is what the doctor said.

There is a cursing word in the Hungarian language that includes the "sacrament" or the "seven sacraments." There is also an internal organ of the human body of which the pronunciation of the Latin name is somewhat similar to "sacrament." I do not know what it is, but I'd heard my father's doctor talking to him about it.

I asked the man to tell me exactly what the doctor had said to him. He could not tell me exactly what the doctor told him; he could only describe what he thought he'd heard. His mind was focused on the word that got him angry without understanding the full statement. He had a prescription in his hand for an anti-inflammatory drug. I explained to him that the doctor's statement meant that he had an inflammation of this internal organ, and the medication was to reduce the inflammation.

When I finished the explanation, all the blood ran out of his face—he got whiter than the white wall. He put his arms around me and thanked me, at least a dozen times, for stopping him from making a terrible mistake.

I hoped that I would never make a mistake like that and, if I did, there would be someone to correct me. I decided to reframe from hasty judgment, particularly if it produced anger.

There was no place at the hospital to keep any personal things, such as my comb, toothbrush, or toothpaste. I had to carry them with me wherever I went. I had a chessboard, and the attendants told me to have it with me at all times, because some of the other people could throw it around and the attendant or I wouldn't be able to do anything about it. So I carried it with me all the time in a bag. I did not have a bed assigned to me and we could not go into the sleeping areas during the day. Bed assignments changed each evening. We had to stay in a common area during waking hours and could not go to the area where the beds were. We were able to watch television and play games or sleep all day long if you felt like it. There were sections in the building where we could go and do some handiwork under supervision. Attendants were present throughout the building at all times to keep order.

There was a music band made up of some of the more permanent residence of the institution. They played at the weekly dance the institution held. It was interesting, because all the permanent residence and people under temporary observation would attend. There I saw a few dozen people who had various types of mental handicaps. These people could not hold jobs or fit in with outside society. There were also young people whose minds were altered by excessive recreational drug use. Some of them told me about the pleasure they got out of these substances. I never had the inclination to use cocaine, heroin, marijuana, or any other hallucinatory chemicals. I had a good opportunity to observe several people who were mentally damaged because of excessive use of narcotics or alcohol.

I remember one time I walked in front of the television and obstructed the view for a second of a fellow who was watching it. He jumped up and attacked me. He wanted to grab my neck. The two attendants present quickly subdued him. He was an overbearing, large person with a violent nature. He seemed to think he knew the answer to everything. After this incident, he was transferred to the fourth floor, where people with more violent behaviors were kept.

There was another fellow, I'll call him Jack, though it is not his real name. We became fairly good friends. We were out in the field one day, sitting on benches, while watching the preliminaries to a softball game. The music band started to play the national anthem. The supervising attendants asked everybody to stand up. Jack would not stand up. He would not stand up when the attendant asked him a second time. The attendant did not ask him again. The next day, he was transferred to the fourth floor too. He spent about a week up there. One had to follow instructions and attendants' requests; otherwise, it was interpreted as unacceptable, uncooperative behavior. There were many young people in the hospital with all kinds of problems, such as alcohol and drug addictions. There were also people who could not find jobs and stress got to them. Life was not easy for many people in New York City.

There was a young electrical engineer on my floor. He told me that he objected to organized religion. I did not want to know what else he objected to. He got a job washing dishes in the kitchen, where the food for the attendants was prepared, and asked me if I would like to work there. He said you can get better food down there. I said yes. The next day I went down with him to talk to the kitchen manager—a good-looking, nice woman in her late thirties or early forties. She talked to me for fifteen to twenty minutes and welcomed me to the group. There were several women and men lined up to do the work and fill in if someone did not show up or did not come anymore.

She started to like me and asked me if I would like to go home with her. I said yes. I was a kind of trilled with the idea, because I liked her a lot too. She had a good-looking body. She went and asked whomever she had to ask to let me go home with her permanently. She told me that her request had been denied. I think she wanted me to live with her, but it was not meant to be.

I met four Hungarian attendants who worked in a different building. One of them told me he worked in the building where the criminally insane people were housed. The others worked in a more peaceful environment with the older people. These Hungarian attendants wanted to take me out and help me find a job. They were told they would have to petition a court. I told them to forget it.

There were a few helping hand held out to me; I just could not hold on to them. It was not time yet. It was like a bad cold. It had to run its course.

I had a hearing about a month or a month and a half after I arrived at the hospital. The floor attendant told me to go to a room where some doctors wanted to talk to me. I went into the room. There were about ten people sitting on one side of a long table. Doctor Ordonez, my doctor, was there among the group, and the Hungarian doctor was sitting at one end of the table. They asked me to sit on the opposite side of the table, across from the ten doctors. I sat down on the chair across from one of the women.

She asked me, "What is wrong with you?"

"Nothing," I said.

Then she asked, "Why are you here? Did something bother you?" She picked up a piece of paper and read it. Then she said, "In this paper, a sentence says that you said that there was a machine lying about you. Do you remember making that statement?" The Hungarian doctor then cut in and asked me in Hungarian if I knew why I was there.

I said, "No, I do not know. And, no, I do not remember saying that." Suddenly I realized that my lack of good English language skills got me into this problem.

That concluded the interview. The final decision was that they would keep me for another two weeks. In the meantime, they would talk to the WWCC to help me get a job.

After I went back to my room, I thought about the statement she'd made to me about the machine. I suddenly realized that there had been a gross misunderstanding of what I'd said and what that woman thought she heard. She decided that I was schizophrenic, I learned later on.

There was an old saying in Hungary that applied to men only: You cannot pee against the wind. It will carry it back on you. I think MDs have the highest egos among all educated people. They are so highly educated, that they are out of touch with common men. They very rarely would admit that they made a mistake. It appeared to me that these MDs did not know anything about the lie detector, and it would be the biggest mistake on my part to try to explain it to them, since I did not know anything about it either. I figured if they thought something was wrong with me, they would also find that they had cured me, and that would be the end of it.

I'd heard of a man from China who'd spent seventeen years in an institution, because he did not speak good enough English to explain himself clearly to those highly educated doctors. They were looking for medical problems where there were really just language barriers and cultural differences. They realized after seventeen years that the man was from a different culture and they just did not understand him. That did not speak well of the medical profession.

I remember there was a picture on the wall of one of my father's doctors that depicted how patients viewed their doctors. When the person was very ill, he viewed the doctor as a God. When the person was getting better, he viewed the doctor as an angel. When the person was cured, he viewed the doctor as an ordinary man. When the doctor gave him the bill, he viewed the doctor as the devil.

There was an incident once when one of my father's doctors prescribed a medication for him that was a combination of different drugs and had to be prepared by the pharmacist. The prescription called for my father to take one tablespoonful three times a day. The pharmacist called the doctor to tell him that the prescription was not safe—it was too toxic. The doctor said to the pharmacist, "It will either cure him or kill him." The pharmacist told this to my father and asked him to take only one teaspoonful or less of it and see how it worked. One teaspoonful of the prescription made my father very sick, and he never took any more of it and never went back to that doctor again. This doctor should have been indicted for attempted murder, but nobody ever took action against him.

My father had an acquaintance who was diagnosed in a hospital with some fatal disease. He asked the doctors, "How long time do I have to live?"

One of the doctors said, "About six months."

He had a lot of wine in the cellar, so he asked the doctors, "How long do I have to live if I drink?"

"About three months," the doctor answered.

The man went home and got drunk every day in the wine cellar. About six months later, one of the doctors met his wife in the market and asked her, "How is your husband?"

"He is drunk in the wine cellar," she said.

He said to her, "Ask him to sober up and come to the hospital. We would like to examine him."

He did sober up and went to the hospital. The doctors could not find any sign of the disease.

He used to brag that his wine was his best medicine. Take this with a grain of salt.

One evening while I was lying in bed, the spirits' voices came back to me and asked me to go over the good things I'd done in my life. I questioned them, "Why are you tormenting me?" There was no answer. There was silence. I thought about a time I rode my bicycle ten kilometers in heavy rain to get a veterinarian for some people, because their cow was sick. I helped people with their farmwork. I was scanning my life in my mind for more examples, when suddenly a vision of a grave site appeared. The floodgate of my memory opened up. I was experiencing myself kneeling at this grave site. My heartbeat increased. The dust has settled on this incident a long, long time ago. I never thought that I'd ever have to go back to it.

It just so happened that the school I was going to was in the city of Székesfehérvár, where the grave of István Kaszap was located. He was a dedicated priest, who'd had ill health and died fairly young. There were stories that miracles used to happen to people who prayed at his grave; they were cured of illness. My fathers had a very bad asthmatic condition, and the doctors he went to could not help him very much. His doctor recommended that he go to the grave of István Kaszap and maybe, by some miraculous way, he would be cured. My father was not very religious and never went there.

When I left for school, I knew that I'd left my father, my mother, and my younger brother in a very difficult situation. It was just after harvest. The field had to be plowed and the seeds had to be returned to the ground for the next year's crops, farmwork that would be very difficult for a woman or an unhealthy man. My mother would never be able to plow the field. They would have to hire someone to do it or ask some of our relatives to help out. I knew my older brother would be out of the army within a month. Deep down in my heart, I knew they would be okay. Regardless, when I went to school, the first thing on my agenda was to visit that grave. The following prayer was left by me at the grave of István Kaszap:

> Please do not let my father die.
> Put part of the burden of his sickness on my back to carry.
> Help my brother to get out of the army.
> Give my mother and father help and enough strength to carry on until my brother gets back home.
> Make me smart, so I can complete my schooling with good grades and can go on the university to become a chemist.
> Please help to end the communistic system in Hungary.

I did not really think about whether or not these things would ever take place. I prayed, and I soon forgot all about it. The consequences of this praying never entered my mind.

I remembered reading about Socrates, who was also advised by spirits. When the court sentenced him to death and asked him to drink the poisonous hemlock solution, he asked the spirits for advice—but his spirit guides were silent. The decision was left up to him.

The decision was left up to me as well. I was looking for some verifiable connection in my mind.

My father had to give himself injections for asthma attacks. The injections had to be given under the skin. If the medicine went directly into the bloodstream, it would kill him He used to give himself the shots into his thigh. Over the years, he gave himself so many injections that his thighs looked greenish, yellowish, and bluish. The skin on his thighs became hard, and he had difficulty finding a place where he could push the injection needle easily into the skin. My father wrote me once that after one of these injections, he was paralyzed for about two or three hours. I guess he got some of the drug into his bloodstream. Maybe he did not die because of my praying. I used to have lots of trouble with my stomach and knees and with headaches when I was in school; maybe this was because I asked to carry some of my father's burden. I graduated as the top student among the 950 students. This result, as well as my brother getting out of the army within three weeks, could have been linked to my praying. I thought, *Five out of six is not bad.*

I was not really convinced that my present situation had anything to do with my praying at that grave. I'd forgotten about God, heaven, and hell long ago. These were not important to me anymore. But just in case, if there was even the slightest chance of a connection, I had to set the record straight. At least I could then say I did it and there was no connection. I didn't even know if I'd be able to tell the difference.

I wrote a letter to my mother. In that letter, I asked her to go to the grave of István Kaszap and ask him to take back all that he had given me. I really did not want to lose my knowledge, but it was a package deal. I was willing to part with everything I'd received, if anything, just to set the record straight in my mind and in reality. The burden was getting too much to carry. I said, *Let nature take its course.*

I was told by someone in the institution that the doctors read all the letters the patients wrote and sent out. I presume they read mine too. They never asked me about it. Maybe that was because it had to do with higher authority, and they did not want to deal with it.

There is a saying. Everything happens for a reason and usually for the better. I just had to learn to tolerate my situation. I slept in a different bed and a different room almost every night. I noticed many times that the bed was soaked with urine from the night before. Once I complained to the staff, "The bed is wet."

I was told, "There is no other bed available." He said, "I would turn it over, but the other side is worse." I had to get used to too many things in that place.

There were several people I played chess and different types of card games with. We were allowed to go out into the field. The field was very large with a tall fence by the road. Another fellow and I used to hit golf balls without endangering anybody by hitting them over the fence, even when we took a full swing with the clubs. There was a baseball field, a cement shuffle board, and some tennis courts. There was also a wooded area with tall trees and bushes.

I had what the doctors called a ring worm infection on the skin on my butt for over a year. I got this after the poison ivy episode, and it seemed to be spreading and was very itchy. I used to sit on the hot radiator edge. The heat seemed to relive some of the itch. I went to several doctors; the solutions they gave me reduced the itch but never totally cured it. I went to see another doctor in the institute with the same symptoms, because the itch was getting worse and it was spreading to a considerably larger area, almost covering my entire buttocks. This doctor gave me the same pinkish solution, judging from the color and the fact that the name seemed to be familiar. I was transferred to another section of the hospital where most of the people were up in age and they all seemed to have some sort of physical problem.

There was a very good checker player among these people. He was a younger person. I would play checkers with him several hours a day. I do not think I ever won a game, but I liked it. He taught me a lot good techniques. I was a chess player at heart, but I learned to like to play checkers.

I met the Hungarian doctor again while I was in this ward. "How are you doing?" he asked me.

"I am doing okay." I told him about my itchy rump and that the medication the doctor gave me does not really do the job of curing it. "I want to ask you a few questions," I said.

"Go ahead, ask," he said.

"They are giving me a tablet. I do not know what it is for. Why do I have to take this medication?" I asked.

"The doctors think you need it," he said.

"What happens if I do not take it?"

"They probably would force you to take it," he said.

"That is interesting," I said. "Why was I transferred to this section with all these old people?" This was my last question.

"This is the rule. They cannot let you go until that itch is cured," he said.

"I've had this thing for over a year. Am I going to be stuck here forever if they cannot cure it?" I asked him.

He shrugged his shoulders and did not say anything and then left. He must have gone to the director of the institution and spoke up on my behalf. Two days later, the doctor who had given me the medicine came to me and was very angry, almost furious. He raised his voice and asked, "Why did you have to talked to the other doctor ? Why didn't you talk to me? You could have talked to me, you know!"

I was surprised by his outburst. "You do not understand me," I said to him. "I do not speak good enough English to explain myself clearly. He is Hungarian, and there is no language problem. There is a big misunderstanding here."

He looked at me, lowered his voice, and said, "Okay, all right."

A few days later, I saw a man who was about five feet tall and was wearing a white uniform. At first I thought he was an attendant. He came over to me and introduced himself as Dr. so and so (I do not remember his name anymore). I introduced myself as Jeno Papp.

"What seems to be wrong with you? Why did they transfer you here?" he asked me.

"I have this nasty itch on my rump," I said.

"Come with me," he said. He took me into an empty examination room. "Take off all your clothes," he said. I got undressed.

He looked at my body. "Let me see. Bend down," he asked me. I did that. He looked at my rump for a minute and said, "How long have you had this? It seems to be spreading."

"Oh, over a year or so," I said.

"I know what this is. It is almost impossible to be cured permanently," he said. "It itches badly, doesn't it?" he asked me.

"Oh, yes," I replied.

He said, "I was in the army during the war," I presumes he meant the Second World War, "and I saw two soldiers that were infected with this. They had it over most of their bodies. They said that it was driving them crazy. No medication seemed to help them. After about two months of trying different treatments, I decided to burn it off."

I thought for a second, *Does he mean with fire?*

"But, then," he continued, "I took a few bottles of iodine tincture and painted their bodies brown with it every day for two weeks. The infection was gone after two weeks. I have not seen happier people since. I will treat you the same way. Wait here. I'll be right back," he said and then left.

He came back with a bottle of dark iodine tincture and some cotton swabs. "Lean down on the table," he said. He painted my body for about five minutes. The burning sensation of the iodine felt wonderful, as it was reducing the itch. "Let it dry for about ten minutes, and then you can get dressed. I will do this again tomorrow at ten o'clock in the morning," he said.

He treated me for two weeks, every day at about ten o'clock. Three days after the two weeks of treatment ended, he examined me again and he said, "It is done. You do not need more treatment. If it ever comes back, you know what to do—treat it the same way as I did."

"Yes, sir! I sure will," I reply to him. I shook his hand and thanked him from the bottom of my heart for freeing me from fifteen months of itching misery. I wished him good luck in wherever he goes and whatever he does.

I had to come to this place where the person was who could cure my ailment. The spirits sent me there for this reason. The rash came back two or three times over the next five years, but I always had a bottle of iodine at hand.

A few days after the doctor cleared me, I went back to my original ward. About a week later, on a Friday, I was told that on Monday they let me go. I told my friend Jack that I was leaving on Monday.

"Do you have any money?" he asked me.

"No, I don't have any, not even a penny," I replied.

He opened his wallet and gave me five dollars. He then said, "They will give you five dollars when you leave, and you will have ten."

A few days before I left, I had a conversation with a man who had just been admitted into the ward. He said he had been there before, and they'd let him go about four months earlier. He told me that he heard voices that told him to go to Alaska for a job. He went to Alaska, but he could not find the job. He could not find a job in the New York area either. He told me other things too, but I cannot remember anymore and I really do not want to remember. He came back and signed himself into the institution, because he said he was still hearing voices and he wanted it to stop. I do not know and never asked him how he was hearing these voices. Was it something similar to what I had gone through? I did not mention to him or to anybody ever the voices I used to hear. I wondered just what kind of a private misery he was living in. I didn't want to know, and I really didn't want to elaborate on it. I had many months of experience with this type of situation, and I have some idea how to deal with it. But that was always very personal.

On Monday morning, after breakfast, the doctor called me into his office and gave me my discharge papers and a prescription for the medication he wanted me to take. He told me that all my immigration identification documents and my social security cards were sent to the Immigration and Naturalization Services in Hartford, Connecticut. The reason for that was my cousin William Papp lived in Fairfield, Connecticut. My cousin and his wife came to visit me once.

The doctor told me to go to the World Wide Catholic Charity Organization in New York City and they would help me get a job. Finally he asked me, "Do you have money?"

I said, "Yes. I have five dollars that my friend Jack gave me."

"Good," he said. But they did not give me any more money. I was disappointed but kept my mouth shut.

He shook my hand and said, "If you have everything, you can go. Good luck to you."

I met a security guard on the way out, and he asked, "Are you going home?"

"Yes," I said. *I am going somewhere*, I thought to myself.

He waved his hand toward me and said, "Good luck to you."

"Thank you," I said. *I will need a lot of it*, I thought to myself.

Interestingly, when I left I did not think of telling the lady manager of the kitchen who had wanted to take me home with her that I was getting discharged. Two years later, I wondered what would have happened if I had told her, "I can go home with you now." Deep down in my mind, I knew I did not want to depend on anyone except myself. I wanted to deal with all the events alone.

In hindsight, the spirit world had a different plan for me.

Chapter 30

Back to the Asphalt Jungle

I left the institution at about eleven o'clock in the morning with two suitcases and a duffel bag. I went to the Long Island Rail Road station and took the train to New York City. I arrived to the Pennsylvania railroad station in the city in the early afternoon. I took the subway uptown to the Hungarian restaurant on Broad Street, where I used to eat frequently when I was at Columbia University. When I got off the subway, I had difficulty carrying my three bags up the steps leading to the street. People were rushing by me and bumping into each other. I noticed that there was a priest about sixty feet away who was coming straight to me. This situation stuck in my mind, because it looked to me like somebody told him to come to me. It may have been his kindness directing him or maybe something else, some spirit from the spirit world.

As he came to my side, he asked me, "May I help you with your packages?"

"Yes," I said.

He picked up the largest suitcase and carried it up the steps. We came up the stairs to the street, and he asked me, "Do you need help getting somewhere?"

"No, thanks," I said. "I am going to a restaurant just around the corner." It was next to the exit.

They greeted me with a big "Hello, and how are you doing?"

as I entered the restaurant. The owner of the restaurant said to me, "We have not seen you for a while. Where have you been?"

"I was out of town. I was in Chicago and on Long Island," I said.

I asked them if I could leave my suitcases there for the night, because I knew I was going to have to sleep on the subway or at a bus or railroad station. I did not want any baggage with me to look after.

I was in the college of hard knocks. I was ready to tackle the beast of the jungle—the asphalt jungle, that is. I spent most of the night on the subway, riding back and forth from Brookline to Bronx.

I went to the World Wide Catholic Charity organization early the next day. They put me up in the same hotel on 31st Street in Manhattan and sent me to the state unemployment office. I got a job within a week at a wire company. The company was producing, among other things, wire racks that were used to display paperback books for sale in stores.

Six other young Hungarian men were working there too. Two of them got a nickel raise per hour in pay. Two of the others went to the owner and asked for more money. Instead of giving them more money, the owner took away the nickel raise from the other two people. It was a cutthroat job.

I and another person were putting these racks into boxes. This person knew tricks on how to get promoted or get a better position. Whenever the manager was not around, he said, "Don't work so hard. Slow down." When the manager was around, he kept saying, "Work faster. You work too slow." I asked the supervisor if he knew of anyplace where I could get a job in the field of chemistry.

The company wanted my social security identification card, and I did not have it. It was still at the immigration office in Hartford Connecticut. I went up there and got it, along with the rest of my papers. I showed it to them.

The result of all these things was they let me go. I became the victim of a dirty trick the man played on me to advance his position. I knew I was on the right track of life. Things were going bad like before. I had to move on. Well, I was on my way to fame and fortune. I would wait for both!

Within a week, I went to work on a mink farm in Green Lawn, Long Island. It was owned by a pharmacist who was teaching at Brookline College. I was living in the same house with him and his elderly parents. I was in charge of feeding the mink and cleaning the cages. I thought I was wasting my life away by looking after future fur coats. I got fed up with feeding mink; therefore, I only stayed for about two months and then left.

After that, I got a job washing dishes at a Howard Johnson restaurant in Hicksville, Long Island, for about two months. I was constantly looking for a job in the field of chemistry.

I had a room in the house of an old lady. She used to tell me that all the space explorations were fakes. "They are doing it in the deserts of Arizona," she would say. I could not change her mind about that. To her, it was impossible to land on the moon. She was probably not the only one who thought this.

I finally got a job in a fiberglass manufacturing company in the Bronx. I was helping a Swiss mechanical engineer do research. He was working on a continuous fiberglass sheet extrusion machine. The aim was to produce a much harder surface for the fiberglass than was available on the market. I lived three blocks from where I worked.

Chapter 31

Letter of Confirmation

I t was during this time, I received a letter from my mother. The letter had been written several months before. It was making its way from address to address, and finally the US Immigration Office sent it to me after my last address registration. I was very grateful for that. I said, "Yes, they do seem to care about us refuges."

This letter could not have been lost. It was under the supervision of spirits. This is what she wrote:

> I did what you asked me to do. I took the train to Székesfehérvár. As I got off the train, an older woman walked up to me and said, "You are Mrs. Papp, aren't you?"
>
> I said, "Yes."
>
> "You are coming to the grave of István Kaszap, aren't you?"
>
> I said, "Yes."
>
> The woman said, "Come with me to my place. You can eat with me and sleep there tonight, and tomorrow I will take you to the grave and you can do what you came for."
>
> I stayed and ate at her home. The next day we

went to the grave, and I did what you asked me to do. The woman came back to the railroad station with me, and I came home.

She also asked me in the letter:
How did she know who I was?
How did she know what I was coming for?
How did she know what train I was coming on?
She seemed to recognize me, and she seemed to know why I came there.

I never answered her questions. I did not want to tell my mother what this situation was about. No one knew anything about my original praying. And the less my mother and anybody else knew, the better off she and everybody else were.

A chilling sensation went down my backbone, and tears came to my eyes. It was scary. Yes, there was a connection between my praying at that grave and what happened to me for the six years that followed it. This was the incident by which I was able to tell the difference. Yes, there was a contract, and it was good until canceled. I was the originator, and I had to cancel it.

I wondered about what kind of forces were at work. I did not want to speculate too much about it at that time.

This old lady must have been in communication with the spirit world just like I was. She must have been advised by the spirit world of my mother's coming. The lady must have been told by the spirits the time of the train arrival and where my mother would be coming out from. The spirits must have pointed out my mother to her. The lady must have been told by the spirits how to treat my mother.

I was too busy getting my life back in order by getting a job I liked, and so I moved on.

The contract had to be canceled. My father had to move on to that other world the spirits were telling me about. One cannot live forever in this time and place. They were preparing me to do what I had to do to accept the inevitable. The only reason I'd asked to take all of it back was because of the communication with the spirits. I had to do this with a clear conscious mind, not with excitement, not with fear, and not with being depressed. That is why I had to go over my past experiences, to set all my feelings of all incidents at an even keel. Whatever I chose I had to live with. I didn't realize the importance, the consequences, and the results of my praying at the grave when I did it.

The realization frightened me. I had to reorganize my thinking and my approach to things I wanted to do. The old adage still echoes in my mind: be careful what you ask for, you might get it.

It was the first day of the rest of my life, which was totally different. My approach to life had been totally changed. I searched in my mind through the time period I'd spent at the university in Budapest to see if there was anything else I had to correct. Interestingly, the urge to correct something was gone. The correction had been made.

My father passed away within a year. My mother told me in her letter that my father's last words were, "I am going to my son to the United States."

My mother passed away the following year from cancer and from a broken heart. They were tied together by an unbreakable bond. My father's death probably accelerated the spreading of the cancer in my mother. She never knew the reason for what I'd asked her to do.

I understand the ability of the spirit world to communicate. Just what are these forces that exist and have control beyond our everyday perception? I thought about this for many years. It scared me for the rest of my life.

I did not realize my praying at that grave was going to be good until canceled. Maybe it was better that I was ignorant of it.

The communication between the spirits and me tapered off. The spirits would get in touch with me only when there was something I had to know that was not on the immediate agenda. I was in good hands, but I had to be responsible for my actions to the laws of the land. I learned to look at the price tag for all my actions. There is a price tag attached to everything we do. There were a few things in my mind that I had to alter and revise. There is a saying that it is not the news but how you respond to it that is important. Foreseeing the future is very difficult on the emotions of a person.

The spirits asked me not to write about this until I was an old man. I ignored their request and I tried to write about it several times, but a fear gripped my mind and I'd have to abandon my efforts. I learned why I could not write about it as time went on. I didn't know the true meaning of the entire situation. I used to think I was the focal point and I was controlling the situation. After many, many years, I finally realized the spirit world was the focal point. The spirits were running the show. I was just an actor having a part in it. I believe the spirits were with me when I was born, and they will be with me when I take my final exit from the human race. They were escorting me through the treacherous roads of human life.

It took me fifty-some years to partially understand the relationship between the spirit world and the biological system that exists on this earth. We are insignificant beings, making a lot of noise and trying to control everything without learning the rules. I do not know if there is any higher spiritual leadership in the spirit world.

The human body is a congregation of various living microorganisms and various chemical elements. The spirit is just imprisoned in it and learning independence. As a spirit, one must learn the rules of how to rebuild your body and avoid self-destruction. All human beings are here by choice or by being forced to be here. You cannot have a servant constantly looking after you ensuring that nothing goes wrong. If you are in constant need of a servant or an overlord to look after you, then you are not yet capable of universal existence. To learn and to accept independence is a very big task for any human being. It means giving up the comfort zone and challenging the unknown. You have to make sure you know what you want and learn how to achieve it. All human beings are traveling different roads of development. They should not be herded by force of an organization into all adhere to the same behavior.

The spirits talked about the development of different human beings who can repair their human bodies without outside assistance. I assume they were referring to spirits that resides in the human body. This involves teleportation of matter, molecules, and atoms. It requires the change of social structure of the human race. I am not sure when or if this human race will ever be ready to make such a change. Lots of changes in honesty, caring, sharing, and helping each other will have to be addressed.

Human bodies are renewed in the form of newborn children. They are born, grow up, get old, and die and leave nothing behind. They take with them, in the spirit form, what we teach them or what they learn. If we teach violence, hatred, revenge, or greed, that is what they teach to their children. Help each other to move forward in development.

The earth, too, has a limited time of existence. The sun is on a set course to become a red giant and take everything with it from the solar system. Once the earth is gone, all spirits will be dispersed into the universe. They are going to have to use the knowledge they have acquired to make a new home somewhere.

Chapter 32

Recommendations

Human beings have to make choices about what they want to be and work at becoming it. If you want to be a murderer, nature will support you to become one—but the price tag is very high on it. Anger, hatred, jealousy, greed, and obtaining anything when you have to hurt someone should not be your driving force. You are going to have to pay the price somewhere along the way. Knowledge that you can take with you to the other side is the only important thing. Do not ask the spirit world to do things for you that you can do yourself. They are not your servants. Get yourself in gear and do it.

One cannot share the suffering of another person in the past. The past is gone, and that is that. I could not have shared the suffering of Jesus in the hands of the Romans. No one has to abuse oneself to show solidarity, sympathy, and share the suffering of another person in the past.

There is constant change and knowledge being gained by the human race. People should update themselves with it. If the people had not updated their knowledge in the past, we would still be swinging from the trees.

Communication with the spirit world is very personal. One has to do his or her own request. It should be in detail, and the consequences of it should be fully realized before the request is made. You cannot pay someone to pray for you while you go on vacation and have fun.

Do not accuse anyone of anything they did not do. This is a criminal behavior even if it is not prosecuted.

About the Author

This book is about an extremely important part of my life. I made a request from the spirit world in the fall of 1952, and I forgot about it. It turned out to be a contract. The spirits came to visit me in 1958 and gave me an impression that I had to correct something. The contract was so delicate that they never told me what had to be corrected. I had to find it myself in the dusty road of my past life. This book is about the search for the correction.

I was born in Hungary in 1933. I immigrated to the USA in January of 1957. I live in East Windsor, New Jersey. I am a retired research chemist; I worked fifteen years in the flavor and perfume industry and twenty-four years in the pharmaceutical industry.

CPSIA information can be obtained at www.ICGtesting.com
Printed in the USA
BVOW070202190413

318563BV00002B/2/P